Roses for Hedone

Published by 404 Ink Limited
www.404Ink.com
hello@404ink.com

All rights reserved © Prishita Maheshwari-Aplin, 2025.

The right of Prishita Maheshwari-Aplin to be identified as the Author of this Work has been asserted in accordance with the Copyright, Designs and Patent Act 1988.

All rights reserved. No part of this publication may be: i) reproduced or transmitted in any form, electronic or mechanical, including photo-copying, recording or by means of any information storage or retrieval system without prior permission in writing from the publishers; or ii) used or reproduced in any way for the training, development or operation of artificial intelligence (AI) technologies, including generative AI technologies. The rights holders expressly reserve this publication from the text and data mining exception as per Article 4(3) of the Digital Single Market Directive (EU) 2019/790

Please note: Some references include URLs which may change or be unavailable after publication of this book. All references within endnotes were accessible and accurate as of March 2025 but may experience link rot from there on in.

Editing: Heather McDaid
Proofreading: Laura Jones-Rivera & Heather McDaid
Typesetting: Laura Jones-Rivera
Cover design: Luke Bird
Co-founders and publishers of 404 Ink:
Heather McDaid & Laura Jones-Rivera

Print ISBN: 978-1-916637-10-8
Ebook ISBN: 978-1-916637-11-5

EU GPSR Authorised Representative
LOGOS EUROPE, 9 rue Nicolas Poussin,
17000, LA ROCHELLE, France
E-mail: Contact@logoseurope.eu

Printed and bound in Great Britain by Clays Ltd, Elcograf S.p.A.

404 Ink acknowledges and is thankful for support from Creative Scotland in the publication of this title.

LOTTERY FUNDED

Roses for Hedone

On Queer Hedonism and World-Making Through Pleasure

Prishita Maheshwari-Aplin

Inklings

Contents

Preamble — i

Introduction
Tradition — 1

Chapter 1
Èros//Exploration — 13

Chapter 2
Philautia//Emancipation — 31

Chapter 3
Paidia//Expression — 49

Chapter 4
Agape//Collaboration — 67

Conclusion
Pragma — 85

References — 95
Acknowledgements — 109
About the Author — 111
About the Inklings series — 113

A love letter to the queer will.

Preamble

1. I use the word *queer* as an umbrella for the LGBTQIA+ community. This includes but is not limited to those who identify as: Lesbian; Gay; Bisexual; Trans; Intersex; Asexual/Aromantic; Pansexual; Genderqueer. Sometimes I use queer and LGBTQIA+ interchangeably, and other times LGBTQ+/LGBTQIA+ refers to the terminology used in a piece of research or by an organisation.
2. My understanding of *queerness* as an identity and experience is built from that as defined by African American feminist author and activist bell hooks. Speaking at The New School in 2014, she described "queer not as being about who you're having sex with (that can be a dimension of it); but queer as being about the self that is at odds with everything around it, and has to invent and create and find a place to speak and to thrive and to live".
3. I write from my personal and queer contextual experience as an Indian immigrant come-of-age in the

UK. As such, while I've ventured to offer global examples to draw intra-community links and highlight boundaryless alignment, this thesis has predominantly grown from the seeds of my own life and those of my peers in Global North and "Westernised" countries.

4. The same applies to the depth and breadth of the LGBTQIA+ community. Within the text's limits, I've tried to provide broad examples – acknowledging the sometimes overlapping but differing experiences of identity groups. This book does not suggest that all queer people have the experiences explored within, or that engagement in these cultures is a prerequisite for a queer identity

5. I speak of heterotopia as a world within a world; a space that reflects the structures and rules of the external world, but exposes, distorts, subverts or dismantles them to create space for something new, something better. This builds on the concept as proposed by philosopher Michel Foucault in his 1984 essay "Of Other Spaces: Utopias and Heterotopias" – as cultural, institutional and discursive space, "counter-sites" to the unreal "utopia", spaces that already exist in societies and simultaneously represent, contest, and invert the norm.[1]

6. This work builds on a shared understanding that liberatory and utopian futures must be anti-capitalist,

anti-colonial, and sustained by mutual accountability and care. This honours the revolutionary thinking of Black and Brown feminist scholars and abolitionists, and queer actionists – Audre Lorde, Angela Davis, Arundhati Roy and Marsha P. Johnson, to name but a few. It's also rooted in the argument posed by Lithuanian-born anarchist Emma Goldman that capitalism is incompatible with human liberty, and that capitalism and colonialism are connected by power.[2]

7. This vision for utopian queer futures is also informed by the values of a pluriverse – one that is radically interdependent and attuned to the Earth – as outlined in the 2019 anthology *Pluriverse: A Post-development Dictionary*.[3] These include, but aren't limited to: solidarity and reciprocity; commons and collective ethics; enoughness; non-hierarchy; and oneness with the rights of nature.

8. *Roses for Hedone* celebrates hedonism as an expansive and joyful pathway to healing, connection and resistance. It does not encourage nor endorse practices that circumvent consent, exploit power dynamics or contribute to systemic harm. This is not to say that queer individuals cannot cause – or have not caused – harm to themselves or to others. Thus, as we engage with the queer tradition of hedonism as a liberatory practice, we also must interrogate in parallel our complicity in proliferating its bad boy image.

Introduction
Tradition

tradition. *From Middle English tradicioun, Old French tradicion, Latin trāditiō; from the verb trādō.* An inherited, established, or customary cultural pattern of thought, action, or behaviour.

Smokey dens draped with delicate limbs; eyelids fluttering as bodies and minds are cast adrift, floating on an endless sea with no horizon. Dark corridors lined with latex, leather, and naked skin; bodies dripping with sweat, writhing and grinding to deep techno; the faint "thwack" of paddles whistling through the pulsating air.

For many, the concept of "hedonism" conjures countless images reflecting an egotistical and self-serving debauchery. Oscar Wilde's 1891 novel *The Picture of Dorian Gray* was published into Victorian Britain with much controversy and was even used as evidence during his 1895 homosexuality trials. In this infamous – and censored – book, the protagonist succumbs to amoral hedonistic temptations and sells his soul in exchange for eternal youth – while his portrait in the attic deteriorates by the hour, bearing the marks of his many sins. F. Scott Fitzgerald's *The Great Gatsby*, too, critiques the hedonism of the Roaring '20s and the American Dream. Motivated by prideful posturing and instant gratification, multiple characters face pitiful consequences. Alcohol, sex, drugs – in much of the mainstream canon, we're confronted by stories of overindulgence, shame, and, ultimately, an inevitable downward spiral.

The word "hedonism" comes from the Greek word for "pleasure", *hedone*, or from *hedys*, meaning "sweet" or "pleasant". Defined as "the pursuit of one's own pleasure as an end in itself",[4] "hedonism" is the process of "living and behaving in ways that mean you get as much pleasure out of life as possible, according to the belief that the most important thing in life is to enjoy yourself".[5] While these definitions suggest a prioritisation of immediate personal pleasure, philosophical schools of thought have raised conflicting psychological and ethical considerations in pursuing a "hedonistic" lifestyle. The earliest form of hedonism as proposed by the Cyrenaic school – active around 3rd century BC – argued that "the goal of a good life should be the sentient pleasure of the moment".[6] While Epicureanism – which emerged in the Hellenistic era lasting between 323–31 BC – argued that "the true hedonist would aim at a life of enduring pleasure, but this would be obtainable only under the guidance of reason", to the extent that some members of the school considered an ideal life to be rooted in indifference to pain, rather than in seeking happiness and enjoyment. In the 18th century, philosopher and economist Jeremy Bentham considered hedonism within his highly influential ethics of utilitarianism, highlighting a paradox that positions an act which one does *thinking* that it will give the most pleasure against the act which one ought to do because it *really will* provide the most pleasure. Others have criticised "hedonism", with 18th century religious thinker Joseph Butler, for example, maintaining that pleasure is only a secondary outcome once a desire has obtained its true object. This theory has, however, not held ground on the basis that we clearly *do* act in ways purely driven by pleasure, such as eating when we're not hungry because it tastes good and makes us feel happy.

The desires that propel us in search of fulfilment are complex and varied – something that philosophers and scientists have been wrestling with for centuries. But, for these purposes, let us begin with the following shared understanding: while hedonism, at its core, is clearly associated deeply with the process of achieving pleasure, our definitions need not limit – or cast judgement upon

– the steps we take to get there. It's also not necessary for this terminology to dictate the kinds of pleasures we can be seeking to experience on the road to happiness.

"Pleasure" in itself is an expansive term with many nuanced layers. Happiness, contentment, ecstasy, tranquility, exhilaration, gratitude – the word holds wide-ranging, and sometimes contradictory, emotions within its folds. Thus, to assume that all hedonism must be purely physical is a perversion of an entirely human pursuit for joy and satisfaction. A pursuit that marginalised communities – those historically erased, oppressed, or exploited by wider society – have often sought as a route by which to survive, connect and even to resist. As adrienne maree brown stated in *Pleasure Activism: The Politics of Feeling Good*: "There is no way to repress pleasure and expect liberation, satisfaction, or joy."

Chasing a high through the industrial landscape of Berlin, you'd undoubtedly be jackhammered by the city's rapid heartbeat – but this heady soundtrack to 21st century European hedonism has its roots in Black resistance. Detroit Techno, the granddaddy of modern techno, was conceived in 1980s Michigan "as a reaction to inner-city decay, as byproduct of African-American struggle, as a form of protest."[7] Elsewhere in the 1980s, as the AIDS crisis devastated the LGBTQIA+ community, grieving gays gathered to party and protest in equal measures. During the 2020 Black Lives Matter protests, non-profit

Fuel the People provided tens of thousands with delicious hot food, ranging from Ethiopian sambusas to Haitian patties,[8] nourishing their aching feet and reviving their passionate chants. Today, children in occupied Palestine perform plays and dance the dabke to cheers that drown out the relentless wails of missiles from above.[9]

There is, of course, inherent value in delight, tranquility, and other such sweet sensations, but what more can we learn about hedonism as a practice when we consider its longitudinal potential energy? How much power can be derived from understanding pleasure to be a cumulative force of our humanity? What if we view hedonism not only in the present moment, but also in the future tense?

In her 1978 essay "The Uses of the Erotic: The Erotic as Power" Audre Lorde frames the erotic not only as a sexual feeling or activity, but rather as a "personification of love in all its aspects".[10] Forming a bridge between "those physical, emotional, and psychic expressions" of love in its deepest meanings, the erotic acts as one resource among "various sources of power within the culture of the oppressed that can provide energy for change". Their potential to empower us and to connect us, Lorde posits, is the very reason that oppressive forces seek to "corrupt or distort" such sources of power.

Indeed, from threats to queer art under Hungary's 2021 anti-LGBT laws to the criminalisation of dance in Iran by the Islamic Republic, authoritarian regimes continue their attempt to suppress personal and shared pleasures with societal shame, legal powers or military action. But, as Newton's third law dictates, for every action, there must be an equal and opposite reaction. While such oppressive forces play their wicked game, a low fire rages at the fringes of our perception. Transient pockets burn bright and sparks jump across valleys to caress waiting fingertips. Fire lilies are ravaged by raging billows, only to bloom once again from the scorched earth. Such is the consistent hum of resistance. The perpetual rebirth of revolution.

The queer community has long practised a reclamation of the "erotic" as a means to live not under, but in defiance of, an oppressive society. While 1960s New York queers sought solace on Fire Island as "a place where hedonism could be balanced with reflection",[11] gay men in India were cruising in the shadows from Delhi to Kolkata; illustrators such as Keith Haring turned their art to activism through the AIDS crisis to create meaning and mobilise change; and today, sober queers gather in London's woods to connect with nature while young Nigerians find belonging through reviving the ballroom scene of decades past. It's our tradition to challenge the status quo, and model more reciprocal, caring and forward-looking ways of living and loving.

So, what is "queer hedonism"? Is it merely the pursuit of pleasure by those who identify outside the bounds of a cis-heteronormative existence? Or is there potential within the folds of the very words that can help us redefine and re-engage with this oft demonised phenomenon?

When practised within an overarching framework and queer intention where individuals seek to "invent and create and find a place to speak and to thrive and to live", our hedonism must, in fact, venture to be harm-reducing. Through reflecting on queer history and experience, we can understand hedonism's role as a source of power that can "provide energy for change" – or even simply a route to survival – for those oppressed by society. It also considers the world-making potential of shared pleasure and places it on par with the desires of the individual. This has been especially true for those most marginalised, especially at times of heightened suffering and oppression.

Furthermore, queer hedonism challenges a capitalist mindset that one perpetually must be chasing the next level of pleasure to achieve true hedonistic enlightenment; to be forever searching for bigger, better, MORE – never content. This impossible chase is the very spiral that leads individuals down to the canonical "dark path" – when nothing is ever enough, how do you know when to stop? How *can* you even stop if you believe you're yet to achieve total satisfaction? Thriving within this uncertainty, queer pleasure-seeking behaviour can create more room to revel in the ephemeral pleasures of the journey.

As writer Jen Winston once mused: "Maybe confusion is as queer as it gets."[12] Sure, the destination's still hot. But queer revelry is about so much more than the climax.

Thus, we arrive at a hedonism that not only offers us liberatory teachings but also operates with consideration for our shared futures. This *hedono-futurism* celebrates the complexities of pleasure; it revels in sweet existence and gasps with orgasmic ecstasy. But it also demands more from us. We're called to interrogate not only the ways in which we find and experience pleasure, but also its impact on ourselves and others. *Hedono-futurism* is not content purely with the synthesis of transient utopic universes as forms of resistance – as crucial as these also may be – but empowers us to transfer modelled learnings and apply them to our real-world interactions and actions.

At a time in my life when all seemed dark, hedono-futurism was the light. I'd always considered myself a hedonist – ripping through the sexual playground of the city, revelling in the sensory satisfactions on offer. But it was only when I found a home amongst the queers-fighting-in-solidarity-with-other-queers that I began to address the trauma stoking the flames of my sometimes-self-destructive hedonistic streak. Organising with grassroots direct-action group for global queer liberation Voices4 London since its inception provided my unruly self with a purpose – it grounded me in something far bigger and more profound than myself. I made the motto "Queers Anywhere are Responsible for Queers Everywhere" my mantra and got "QUEER LIBERATION NOT GAY ASSIMILATION" tattooed on my ankle. I made friendships that held and healed me. But through the rallies and banner-making; the solidarity actions with queers in Poland, Bangladesh, Hungary; the cosy movie nights and the euphoric parties, I found a queerness rooted in care for others – a political home where our love for each other seemed boundless and boundary-less. Vietnamese American poet Ocean Vuong once said that being queer saved his life.[13] I can unequivocally say that it also saved mine.

As I look around me now, I feel so deeply a need for us to shift our relationship with, and understanding of, queer hedonism. Too many of us have held a friend as they k-hole or helped a stranger on GHB leave the dancefloor in one piece. We've watched as loved ones have their hearts broken, and as others risk their safety for a quick shag that leaves them feeling empty. We've all attended one too many memorials for trans women systemically abused and abandoned. It's not enough for us – especially in the Global North as queers with relative privilege – simply to co-opt Black feminist Toi Derricotte's words: "Joy is an act of resistance."

In this day when we face rampant transphobia, rising hate crime, and unequal access to support services – all in the context of humanitarian crises, a climate crisis, and a destabilised political landscape – we must do more than accept neoliberalist identity politics that presuppose utopia on the queer dancefloor. We instead must channel the potential energy that our bodies produce together to prefigure a pluriversal futurity – and to heal, innovate and organise to create it in community. As Larry Mitchell wrote in his 1977 fable-cum-manifesto, *The Faggots & Their Friends Between Revolutions*: "We keep each other alive any way we can 'cause nobody else is goin' do it."[14]

The question I hope now to tackle is what more pleasure can offer us, and how we can transform this pleasure into intentional practice in pursuit of a collective liberatory future.

The "erotic" of which Audre Lorde speaks stems from the Greek word "Éros", the god of love and desire, born of Chaos. But the Ancient Greeks considered the spectrum of love as extending beyond this singular definition, categorising it into at least eight forms: Éros (romantic, sexually passionate and lustful love); Philautia (self-love); Philia (platonic love between friends); Storge (experienced by parents for their children); Paidia (playful love); Xenia (hospitality or guest-friendship); Agape (unconditional, universal or sacrificial love such as between person and God); and Pragma (committed and enduring love). Through this broad exploration, philosophers of the time acknowledged the "materialistic conception of love as purely a physical phenomenon—an animalistic or genetic urge that dictates our behaviour—to theories of love as an intensely spiritual affair that in its highest permits us to touch divinity".[15]

Pleasure can look, feel, smell, taste like countless – sometimes indescribable – sensations. And love and pleasure are deeply intertwined, often developing in tandem. So, let us place our pleasure-seeking behaviours gently into the interwoven baskets of this multiplicity – through Éros, Philautia, Paidia and Agape – as we explore queer hedonism not as a momentary phenomenon, but rather a transformational route through which we connect, grow and resist – together.

Chapter 1
Èros//Exploration

eros. *From Ancient Greek Ἔρως (Érōs). The Greek god of erotic love. Refers to a sexual love or desire; conceived by Plato as a fundamental creative impulse having a sensual element.*

Each year, as London pops under the August sun – the scent of petrichor and the buzz of possibility heavy in the pollen-filled air – gaggles of queers trek to Hampstead Heath and become one with each other and the trees. Yeah, "This is My Culture" is a really good fucking party. Lesbians jelly wrestle topless while an enigmatic maître de soaks them in oil from an emptied bottle of washing up liquid, gays disappear into the trees and emerge tousled and smiling, and the bass thumps while bodies of all shapes and sizes writhe in coordinated ecstasy. But it's also so much more than that.

This annual memorial-slash-protest-slash-party celebrates the life of iconic singer George Michael, and his talent, courage and sexual freedom. It was first hosted to mark the nineteenth anniversary of Michael's arrest in 1998 at Will Rogers Memorial Park in Beverley Hills. His crime? Cruising for gay sex.

From the ancient Roman bath houses to the Jardin des Tuileries in Paris, gay men have rehearsed the art of looking. They've paused, touched and stolen kisses everywhere from the molly houses of eighteenth-and-nineteenth century London – brandy shops, taverns and theatres where "dozens of men would congregate to meet one another for sex or for love" – to rest stops and underpasses in the United States.[16] In 2015, while taking a late-night stroll on Hampstead Heath, George Michael was ambushed by a photographer from News of the World. Unabashed and defiant, he simply snapped: "Are you gay? No? Then fuck off! This is my culture!"[17] True, cruising – the art of searching for sexual partners in public places – is partly about erotic satisfaction. But as Alex Espinoza writes in *Cruising: An Intimate History of a Radical Pastime*: "Cruising is not just about participation in a sexual experience; it is an act that promulgates a unique cultural practice necessary for the survival of the culture as a whole."[18] A cultural practice – an oral tradition, if you will – which creates space for homosexual intimacy within shame-filled and oppressive environments.

Espinoza opens his book by describing this practice as almost meditative. It "teaches you how to be still in the moment, how to feel the Earth spinning on its axis, how to sense the gravitational pull of the ground beneath your feet." Here, there is a pleasure of existence, of mindfulness, that draws our attention from an aspirational erotic climax and into the present moment. It's this indulgence in the process that taught Espinoza patience, perseverance and "how to cultivate a sense of confidence". It's also in these moments between – where the air is ripe with potential – that we learn not only about ourselves, but also how to relate to others with a forward-looking intentionality.

Participating in an act of sexual deviancy allows queer people to autonomously choose what has for so long been imposed upon us. Just as LGBTQIA+ people have reclaimed "queer" as a signifier of acceptance and strength, when we cruise, we shed the shame and revel in our perversions. Through engaging with this queer tradition of low culture – the "trashy" – we convert it into a "high form of disruptive behaviour."[19] We also circumvent capitalist pressures and expectations, for we accept the possibility of failure and "wasted time". As academic Jack Halberstam argues in *The Queer Art of Failure*, a queer failure to live up to heteronormative societal standards of success can prompt us to fall short, get distracted, find a limit and to avoid mastery, among other things – all of which ultimately help us recognise that "empathy with the victor invariably benefits the rulers".[20] In rehearsing the queer art of failure, we losers stand on the shoulders of those who lost before us.

Recognisable through scattered clues, cruising sites offer an erotic paradox akin to Schrödinger's Cat, wherein at any one time there could or could not be the possibility for connection. They blur the binary of *knowing/not knowing*, and imbue every unspoken glance with transformational potential. An almost imperceptible nod; a brief graze of the crotch; a lip bite and a tilt of the head.

This is especially true when coupled with other forms of code. Bob Damron's *Address Book*, a gay yellow pages published in 1965 as a pocket book "so small that it could fit inside the back pocket of a pair of Levi's or Wranglers" listed names of gay bars and "cruisy areas", including a key featuring letters such as "D" for "Dancing" and "RT" for "Raunchy Types".[21] Alongside these listings, Damron also included a detailed explanation of handkerchief colours and their meanings as per the "Hankie Code". According to Damron, a mustard hankie in the right pocket communicated that the wearer wanted 8"+, while a light blue in the left asked for a 69.[22] With time, the more problematic codes have been dropped – some were racist or relayed inappropriate age preferences – and the range of colours and textures expanded.

This queer tradition of codified language and signage is one under which cruising as a practice slots gently. As artist and curator Mac Martin observed in a 2018 interview with *International Business Times*, "These seemingly squalid, gloomy and stinking places were incredible places of social mixing. Homos and straights of all social strata, men of all ages, cultural and religious backgrounds – they all came together there."[23] In 1791 Paris, aristocrats and workers looked to one another for a transient and radical exchange that defied the "normal" rules and expectations of society.[24] Punters in 1934 London from disparate social strata sought membership at the city's "greatest bohemian rendezvous", the Caravan Club.[25] Men of colour, so often fetishised as non-normative partners, speak of using the cruising ground to take control and undermine racialised politics of desire. And trans men experience glimmers of gender euphoria within the shared erotic gaze.[26]

The world-making potential of cruising has allowed this practice to flourish during times and in places of increased stigmatisation, policing and criminalisation. In 18th century London, cruising spots were established around alleyways, arcades and theatres "out of a collective desire to seek out that which was officially taboo."[27] Over 200 years later, photographer Sunil Gupta attempted to document the plethora of gay cruising in public places around New Delhi, at a time when homosexuality was still criminalised. Such was the danger that Gupta had to enlist volunteers to act in his photographs. Today, queer people in countries where even to be perceived as homosexual in public can be life-threatening use VPNs to seek anonymous connections and pre-arranged orgasms via cruising forums and dating apps.[28] Although some purists consider these sites, such as Squirt.org, Grindr or Hornet, not to fall under the definition of "cruising", let's tear down those gates for the sake of our shared understanding and view such activity through the lens of circumstantial safety and aligned intent.

The access to community, intimacy and sex that cruising provides mostly for men who have sex with men can't be ignored within the context of systemic discrimination and oppression. However, the belief that the only reason gays cruise is to access what cannot be accessed through any other route undermines the depth and breadth of this practice. It also ignores the reality of those whose pursuit of freedom is regularly exploited. In 2019, Human Rights Watch reported that gay men were being set up via dating apps in the Russian region of Chechnya during the anti-gay crackdown of 2019.[29] And, in Uganda, a country with one of the world's harshest anti-gay laws, police officers have been going undercover "pretending to solicit sex to lure gay men out and arrest them."[30] On an interpersonal level, the same liberatory touch can cross the line to predatory when driven by shame and entitlement. There also have been reports of higher rates of other offences, such as thefts, robberies and violent assaults going unreported at known cruising sites by victims who don't want to be "outed".

Cruising clearly doesn't come without risks. Yet, countless men around the world continue to look, touch and embrace in and out of the shadows. For this cultural practice is driven not only by desperation but also by the magic that occurs between the lines. Yes, there may be urgency, but this is rooted in an innate human desire for the very belonging and understanding that has been, and continues to be, kept from the queer community by a heteronormative society. There is taking, but there's also reciprocity. It's a reclamation of sexual agency, an act of survival – a protest.

As he gazed at an exhibition about cruising for gay sex in old Berlin toilets, it wasn't the hyper-sexuality of Mac Martin's images that grabbed writer Jeff Leavell, but rather "the golden light that haloed the scenes, the tenderness on the men's faces, the beauty and romance and desire they portrayed".[31] Indeed, when gay friends share their experiences of cruising on London's Hampstead Heath or in the Calanques of Marseille, they focus not on the spilled semen but rather on the intimacy of bodies pressed together as they surf pleasure as one. How they come to experience their own sexuality as a mosaic of all the men they have met and touched, who, along the way, made it okay to be gay. It's this shared joy and erotic pleasure of which Audre Lorde spoke as providing "a source of power in the culture of the oppressed" to build bridges between us and provide the "energy for change", that has not only allowed cruising to persist despite the associated risks, but also to validate and uplift clusters of the queer community.

Although far less recorded in history, women also have partaken in the culture. Along with a women's toilet block in Portsmouth, which was "closed down because it was believed to be an 'opportuning' site", there have been long-standing rumours of cruising at the Ladies' Pond on London's Hampstead Heath, on Fire Island beaches, and at the lakes around Berlin. Yet, this queer ritual has been less accessible for more marginalised parts of the queer community – for example disabled queer people, or Black and Brown folks who are more likely to be profiled by the police. With high rates of gender-based violence around the world, cis men continue to be more safe loitering in public places or meeting strangers alone than cis women or trans people.

So, those driven by the same desires for connection, relation and consummation have prioritised other ways to get their fix. Gaping caverns of lust dripping with sweat; underground pockets of hedonism humming beneath the buzz of the city streets. I'm talking about sex clubs, dungeons and darkrooms.

Some are lined with black leather and latex, some draped in soft pink furnishings – others forgo the frills in favour of a smattering of vinyl sofas and a bowl of condoms and lube. Whether you're slapping cheeks to deep techno, kissing stilettoed feet, or beating your meat to the sound of a hundred moans, darkrooms offer a sense of privacy, safety and control that is impossible to create on the outdoor cruising ground. They also offer a home, and a breeding ground, for another transgressive erotic culture, radical in its subversion and violation of sexual cultural norms: kink.

Written accounts from as early as the Italian Renaissance describe sexual encounters involving pain, suffering and degradation, and it's well-documented that upper-class solicitor Arthur Munbee and his scullery maid Hannah Cullwick were in a consensual Master/slave relationship in Victorian England.[32] Over the course of the 20th century, BDSM as a queer consciousness and subculture evolved in the United States into something visible, potent and far-reaching. The development of gay "leather" culture in 1950s and '60s as an off-shoot of post-World War II motorcycle clubs soon made way for a network of leather bars, fetish publications and kink markets – many using "leather" as a euphemism for their interest in sadomasochism (S/M).[33] By the 1970s, a socio-political movement had arisen around BDSM as a lifestyle, an "open, organized community, which actively sought to teach, connect with, and educate newcomers."[34] Although numerous feminist writers, and gay and lesbian organisations, shunned queer kinksters – connecting BDSM with fascism and labelling it "anti-feminist" and "anti-lesbian" – the fetish community offered a space for erotic exploration and self-expression for those more systemically marginalised. During the 1970s and '80s, dykes in San Francisco founded Samois to challenge limiting ideas around lesbian sexuality and frequented the referral-only S/M fisting club Catacombs.[35]

From tying up a partner and giving or receiving pain, to psychological power exchanges, BDSM – bondage, discipline (or domination), sadism (or submission), masochism – activities fall under a larger umbrella of kinks. These involve intense sensations (pain), sensual experiences connected to erotic targets (fetish) or power differences and expression of power/powerlessness (dominance).[36] Kinks can look like so many things: Dominant/submissive dynamics; foot fetish; voyeurism; role play; giantess fetish – the list goes on. As psychotherapist Douglas Thomas writes in *The Deep Psychology of BDSM and Kink*: "At its root, BDSM is a conscious exercise in the eroticization of alterity."

BDSM dynamics also can model caring, empathetic and reciprocal relational dynamics, and teach us the necessary skills of communication, boundary negotiation and self-soothing. For trans people, queer disabled people and people with certain sensory needs, kink can provide a constructive space to connect with their bodies on their own terms. As Anna Randall, clinical sexologist and executive director of The Alternative Sexualities Health Research Alliance, shared with *Them*, BDSM encourages embodiment, or an intentional connection between the mind, body and senses. This, they noted, can be especially valuable for disabled and/or neurodivergent people, and "can encourage confidence, personal healing, body acceptance, community building and, in some cases, even pain or symptom management."[37] Through this personal healing – not as an individualistic route to detachment from the suffering of others, but rather as a collaborative tool – we become more able to be present and organise in pursuit of collective liberation.

Psychological benefits of BDSM are accompanied also by positive physiological impacts. Studies have found that consensual and pleasurable S/M practices, such as bondage, sensory deprivation, and expressions of caring and affection, can lead to lowered levels of the stress hormone cortisol and feelings of increased closeness between partners.[38] This has also been mirrored by evidence that participation in BDSM creates a pleasurable altered state of consciousness. Here, while the dominant experiences a flow state, the submissive enters what is commonly referred to as "subspace" – a floaty headspace of distorted time, reduced pain and a sense of peace – which parallels often transformational states experienced through meditation and ritual.[39]

For many, BDSM relationship dynamics form around creative and symbolic "scenes" that model intensely human experiences. Consciously and intentionally created with respect for negotiated hard and soft limits, safe words (that can immediately end a scene), clear boundaries and sexual risk awareness, these scenes exist within a "protective container",[40] creating transient and primarily cerebral heterotopias that allow us to explore power struggles, suffering, desperation and devotion outside of society's existing inequalities and violence. It's a useful shorthand to affirm that, in a healthy BDSM practice, nobody is coerced into doing or saying anything they haven't explicitly agreed to beforehand. While not everyone who practises BDSM has experienced trauma, both studies and anecdotes reveal that it can help some to heal from it.

This protective container also allows queers to find erotic pleasure in the transgression of cultural taboos and bio-essentialist gender norms through autonomous self-determination. Through the fantasy and codified language of scenes, queer people can create a reality that may help them survive in a world that erases or vilifies their authentic selves. This is especially true of trans, non-binary and gender nonconforming people, for whom existing in a bio-essentialist and binary gendered society may be unpleasant, dysphoric or simply unbearable. Through kink, trans people can write themselves into the bodies and roles they wish to occupy as they move through the world. If we consider gender as a "constructed identity, a performative accomplishment", as posited by gender studies scholar Judith Butler in 1988, then BDSM scenes provide the perfect backdrop for this play.[41] Just as we embed our gender identity in society through a stylised repetition of acts, we can embody alternate genders within scenes through chosen language, gesture and movement.

For me, submitting to or pledging servitude to another with whom I have built a bond of trust purely because it brings *me* pleasure is radical and freeing in the face of systemic oppression. Choosing to show someone unconditional, almost maternal, care in a world that both rejects and exploits my hypersexualised and pathologised body offers me a route to fulfilment and self-exploration. I'm girl and boy; I'm Mummy and Daddy; I'm princess and Goddess. I am in full control of my destiny and at the helm of the ship that takes me there.

The BDSM of which we speak is not done *to* someone. Instead, it is borne of, and exists within, a safe space created and shared in with consent by two or more people. A space that only exists when we confront our deepest darkest wants and look towards one another, really see one another, and share in the feelings created by our gaze.

Participants of a 2020 study into the experiences of kinky LGBTQ+ people cited their membership in BDSM communities "as a source of great connectedness and solidarity in their lives" that provided a protective buffer against societal discrimination."[42] It was this collective embrace of shared otherness that validated the leather dykes of 1980s London to take up space and powered their political activism. At a time when their sexuality was not only marginalised but actively erased – lesbian activity wasn't even mentioned in the British law that criminalised homosexuality between men until 1967 – the "Rebel Dykes" found one another at Greenham Common Women's Peace Camp. They'd go on to establish Chain Reaction – possibly the world's first-known lesbian kink club. Home to leather nights, fetish performances and mud wrestling, Chain Reaction was a politically-charged reclamation of space. It was pro-sex work and pro-trans. An unabashed celebration of non-binary female sexuality, promiscuity and creativity.

"When we were beating each other and cutting each other, it took the power away from that thing," says Maj Ikal, called Jane Campbell at the time, in the 2021 documentary about their lives, "Rebel Dykes". "Somehow, we felt much more like we could survive a beating."

Through shared eroticism, the Rebel Dykes found a space to process and become more resilient to misogynistic and lesbophobic violence. They challenged the misconceptions and expectations around what sex between two women must look like. They resisted binaries associated with pleasure/pain, embracing two seemingly contradictory impulses through the deliberately ambiguous concept of masochism. They affirmed one another's existence, empowering themselves to transform joy into inspiration and rage into action.

As Audre Lorde shared, acceptance of her inner erotic led her to becoming less willing to accept powerlessness, or other states imposed upon her by external forces, such as despair, self-effacement and self-denial. So it was for the Rebel Dykes, who would go on to campaign with ACT UP to educate on women's experiences with AIDS and, on 2 February 1988, abseil into the House of Lords to protest then-Prime Minister Margaret Thatcher's Section 28 legislation. It was also thus for the leather community in the United States. Not only did individuals give care to HIV-positive community members, but national conferences promoted education, training and social activism "as fundamental elements of an emerging leather culture."[43] Through hedono-futurism, we have long been empowered to demand better for ourselves.

This still rings true. Yet, with shifting socio-political contexts, it's not equally the case for all. With more mainstream acceptance of alternative desires and white homosexual relationships in Western countries, purely the act of engaging in transgressive eroticism is not the radical motion it once was. Pre-AIDS crisis, sex clubs and darkrooms often were places of lawlessness – with free-flowing drugs, shared tubs of lube and no safe words.[44] But with rapid awareness around safer sex also came a growing consciousness, especially among the BDSM community, around the need to create a more holistic safe environment for all. Today, along with making room for consensual exploration of power dynamics, organisations are called to consider their role in actively rejecting all forms of oppression.

Speaking to MJ Fox, co-founder of London-based Joyride – "a space to rave, play and connect" – I'm struck by the intentional steer away from this being purely a sex or play party. Instead, MJ focuses on providing a safer space for people to gather and connect, bonded by a shared interest in erotic pleasure but free to unravel this thread however they like.

"We're a space where people can come and explore their sexuality, their eroticism and also their queerness," says MJ. "We facilitate that space in such a way that people feel calm and comfortable in exploring and expressing themselves in a way that they don't often find in other places."

MJ tells me about a friend who, attending his first Joyride, perceived another member as very good-looking and straight, so dismissed him as a potential playmate.

But, later in the smoking area, discovered they shared many of the same insecurities that had triggered him earlier in the night.

"[They] ended up having this conversation around vulnerability and sobriety. And they really connected in a way that he never thought he could connect with somebody of that disposition," they add. "They've continued to message and to develop this relationship in a platonic sense. That's the real power of what we do."

Joyride is not alone in actively fostering a community around eroticism and kink. With growing consideration for the needs of disabled fetishists, Black and Brown kinksters, and trans deviants, parties such as London's One Night Parties offer a space "where femme-leaning people can meet other like-minded individuals, explore their sexuality or/and develop friendships without feeling any pressure to engage in sex or look a certain way." Kinky Collective, dedicated to promoting and celebrating kink and BDSM culture in India, organised the country's first Kink Con in 2023 – hosting panels, discussions and a kink fashion show. And VoxBody, a rope-dedicated studio in California, centres somatic exploration and a flexible technique that can accommodate a range of bodies, ages and needs.

Through guidelines that are communicated in advance and monitors that oversee the play areas, these events are enacting that a safe space within an unfair and unequal society must be consciously created and upheld, affirming that erotic hedonism that is rooted in values – and, in this case, protocols – does not, and need not, invariably lead to harm. They're acknowledging, "Yes, this is our culture", and it has the power not only to transform the individual, but also to uplift the collective – whether in the smoking area, the playroom or on the dancefloor.

Chapter 2
Philautia//Emancipation

philautia. *Loan from Greek φίλαυτοι, nominative of φίλαυτος, a compound of* phil- +ˈ auto-. *Self-love, self-compassion; a basic human necessity.*

When we speak of nightlife and the role raving plays for the queer community, we say many things. *The dancefloor is refuge. The dancefloor is resistance. The dancefloor is utopia.*

In late 1970s UK, as gays were bashed in the streets and Parliamentary Houses, the party was survival through an affirmative co-existence, sheltered from aggressive external forces. As Jeremy Atherton Lin quoted social critic Michael Warner in *Gay Bar*, "Queer scenes are the true salons des refusés where the most heterogeneous people are brought into great intimacy by their common experience of being despised and rejected in a world of norms that they now recognize as false morality."[45] In the face of overt rejection, these disco-lit worlds were a safer space for queers to revel in the pleasures of a radical self-acceptance – or *philautia*.

In the United States, "circuit parties" had been cropping up from New York to Ohio since the 1969 Stonewall Riots – spreading, growing and evolving, but always in secret, shared by word-of-mouth. While in India, the magic lay in more intimate gatherings – apparently American poet Allen Ginsberg would attend basement parties hosted by local artists and activists in 1960s Kolkata.[46] In the '90s, homosexuality was not only criminalised under a British colonial-era law (only repealed in 2018), but LGBTQIA+ people faced daily harassment, blackmail and ostracism. As activist Arif Jafar shared with *Hindustan Times* in 2023: "In the '90s, no one even wanted to talk to us. If we mentioned being gay, we'd be slapped or abused."[47] Carving out public space for connection, let alone mobilisation, was a challenge when men would be arrested simply for gathering in parks under the allegation that they "were about to indulge in homosexual acts."[48]

Pawan Dhall, co-founder of one of India's oldest queer support groups Counsel Club, hosted his first party in 1994 Kolkata, using his privileges as an out gay man with an accepting family. Although these events were more akin to "school-boy parties", he told me, than sweaty clubs – with food, dancing and PG-13 games – they provided Pawan and his peers with an invaluable form of deep-seated pleasure, validation and self-expression, of flirting openly and innocently, existing among those to whom they didn't need to explain themselves.

We often speak of a queer unravelling of time at a different pace than conventional concepts and understandings. This framework of "queer temporality" interrogates the assumed naturalness of straight time. It also reconsiders how we view concepts of growth such as maturity, responsibility, happiness and future through the lens of fabricated success metrics – still often centred around five "objective" life events ("completing education, entering the labor force, becoming financially independent, getting married, and becoming a parent").[49] Our queer art of failing to "succeed" by heteronormative standards has the potential to open up new pathways down which to invent our futures. So it was for Pawan and his friends, for whom the party offered a refuge within which they could gently tug on the corners of their identities, desires and shared language inside/outside of Indian cultural expectations.

Pawan shared stories from the home of a pilot with whom he was having a brief fling, where a small group of gay men would gather to watch gay pornos from the United States. But rather than dissolving into orgies, they would simply eat, drink and chat. Ultimately, he says, "It was just an occasion to gather, watch the films and then talk about a variety of things." Eroticism as more conventional hedonism was the campfire – almost an excuse, perhaps – around which young gay men could gather. I reflect fondly on how often I've danced underneath giant projections of cock-sucking and finger-blasting vintage pornos at the North London institution, Dalston Superstore. Here, the celebration of our deviancy through gay porn adorns the party in its role as a self-affirming outlet.

The queers sought this refuge again as the world was locked down during the Covid-19 pandemic. Unable to access in-person community and nightlife – and many even forced to move back to their parents' homes where they may have been "in the closet" or regularly misgendered – the party moved online. Thousands around the world joined live-streamed raves on Zoom, all the more accessible and borderless due to their digital form. For me, it was these nuggets of queer joy and release – sequin- and jockstrap-clad bodies and smiling, dancing limbs in tiny squares on my laptop screen – that kept me from burnout as I organised digital days-of-action in solidarity with the Black Lives Matter movement, wrote pieces on racism in the queer community and mobilised against anti-LGBTQ+ zones in Poland alongside a now-Zoom-orientated full-time job, all conducted from my single bedroom at my parents' house. At this time of global grief and trauma, the queer party kept me energised, connected and present.

But sometimes what we need is to be *not present*. Sometimes, the escape we require is not only physical, but also cerebral. Where we can evade the binary of *being/not being*, and exist in freedom even for a moment outside of a body so politicised, demonised and marginalised. In a bid for survival, "disassociation [has become] a gay ritual as much as any other."[50] And with its repetitive beats, smokey air and aura of shared understanding, the queer rave is an ideal situation within which to push out to sea and surrender to the dissociation willingly.

In *Raving*, critical theorist McKenzie Wark explains that trans people tend to be good at dissociation because "we're a kind of people who need to not be in body or world."[51] Dysphoria pushes trans people into dissociation as an escape from this world – but when the world we're escaping is broken, perhaps that liminality is where the answer lies. For Wark, in this "Ravespace", sometimes we "ressociate". We bring the fractured back into alignment; we create a connection or cooperation between discrete parts. For writer and therapist Hannah Baer, dissociation via the snorting of ketamine (k) is a route to seeing herself through a "liberated compartmentalized eye" in all her trans-femininity. She writes in *trans girl suicide museum*: "In my own body too, when I'm on the drug, I feel my own transness, my own capacity for pleasure, my own deep bitch woman cunt femme sassy sister girlness, my angelness, my sweet baby bitchness, all that is tender and beautiful in my fucked up body."[52] K helps Hannah manage what the medical field diagnoses as dysphoria.

As we dissociate, we burst forth in our true forms – the versions that exist outside of societal categorisation. Whether *au naturale* or with a little chemical assistance, we come to float above our bodies and to perceive ourselves as beings beyond our pre-assigned names, sex, gender, nationality. It's like breathing out – or closing your eyes and blowing out hard with your fingers on your nostrils until your ears pop for the tenth time and your head is afloat on a sea of light. But when we open our eyes again, we see only what our minds want/need to see. It's a relief. And, in that moment, as we experience a little death – *la petite mort* – everything is suddenly possible, and ourselves weightless and free.

I explore dissociation's potential as hedono-futurism not to romanticise an extreme survival response. Or to overwrite the fact that this pursuit of cerebral refuge can fuel queer people's unquenchable desire to permanently evade their bodies. But rather to honour Wark's commitment to finding "ways this disability can also be enabling". As a marginalised community with a history of seeking *feeling/ not feeling* in the arms of substances, we're unlikely to stop using all of a sudden. Countless studies have reported higher rates of drug use and abuse by the LGBTQ+ community on a global scale than our heterosexual counterparts.[53] And there are a range of factors that contribute to these figures, from mental health, trauma and dysphoria – to de-stigmatisation of pleasure and life-affirming participation in transhistorical queer subcultures.

As such, I have no desire to promote or demonise drugs – they just *are*. They're a reality of our party culture, they can help us cope and, often, they're fucking fun. So, I move forward with acceptance and with gratitude for organisations promoting harm-reduction and offering support to those struggling with dependency.

The addictive quality of drugs' chemical compounds predisposes them to the endless chase for the next best thing, as does the genetic make-up of some people. Thus, we cannot – and must not – place the responsibility of managing addiction, and reframing hedonism, solely on individuals. But can we venture to create a protective container around this culture which is rooted in the values of intentionality and care? With a lack of mainstream support and tailored services – LGBTQ+ charity Stonewall's 2018 report found that one in eight LGBTQ+ individuals received unequal care, with this number rising to 32% of transgender people – can hedono-futurism help us support ourselves and one another? Can it, in fact, be the transformational route through which we access individual and collective healing in aid of pluriversal futures?

The rave can be where we dissociate but it can also be where we release the trauma that creates the conditions for dissociation. We can let the music fuck it out of us.[54] Our system collects such high levels of stress chemicals that it changes the way our brain processes immediate information. But when I speak with my therapist, I notice how my body physically expels stress. On the dancefloor, I notice the same release. As my friends and I dance to ASHTREY's set at the Cause in East London, I yawn as the ritualistic rhythms loosen the tension in my lower back. And I think about the long history of dance as healing practice among ancient cultures, such as the Hoop Dance, a choreographed prayer practised by a number of Indigenous peoples of the Americas, which offers individual and collective healing through a manifestation of togetherness.[55] Indeed, a one-hour set can take us on a journey of *push/pull, rise/fall* – where we float and sink in tandem/synchronicity – and experience something akin to *euphoria* (the Greek word describing a state of good health); to the *xeno-euphoria* described by Wark; or even *eusexua*, coined by multi-disciplinary artist FKA Twigs to encompass a state of total sensual wellness, inspired by feelings of gratitude and aliveness that she experienced at a rave in Prague.

It's not uncommon for fellow queers to refer to the rave as "a religious experience". It's a church for the sinners, needy for connection and purpose. Sociologist Amin Ghaziani says in *Long Live Queer Nightlife*: "We form attachments with other people as we hang out with them here at a gay bar, or there at a club night. Place matters." Just as music helps religious communities experience higher levels of meaning, so can our worship at the altar of the DJ – promoting "spontaneous unscripted conditions for group pride, communal attachments, and feelings of belonging."[56] And when we dance with energy and synchronicity – when we side-step and pump our shoulders as one – our bodies release endorphins that inspire positive feelings towards one another and elevate our pain threshold.[57] In a sense, the rave makes us literally more able to withstand the pain from queerphobia and queer bashing.

The party also offers a physical space to bring the ephemeral into the material. Indeed, there's much interdisciplinary scholarship that highlights the importance of dance as a resistance culture and heuristic device in places and periods of conflict – from the opening of a ballet school in Gaza and the birth of an innovative dance music scene in Sarajevo during the war in Bosnia, to the transnational connections mediated through hip-hop in post-war Iraq.[58] Through dancing as a form of agency that allows us to claim a personhood beyond that of "the oppressed other", we're able to access embodied resistance beyond escapism – propelling us forward "beyond romances of the negative and toiling in the present".[59] And by sharing in this *ekstatis* as a conduit for collective temporal distortion, we disrupt hopeless inevitability and create active pathways to new and better futures.[60] It's also through this lens that we can consider the subcultural significance of queer drug-use and the parameters for resilience and resistance held within this practice.

Drugs, especially psychedelics, can enact a queer futurity by prefiguring the pluriversal futures we aim to create together. Indeed, in many Indigenous cultures, such as communities in the western and north-western Amazon and practitioners of the Bwiti religion in Gabon, Central Africa, hallucinogenic plants are traditionally consumed to access ancestral knowledge, individual spiritual growth and community strengthening. As Foucault explored in a 1971 interview: "Deep down, what is the experience of drugs, if not this: to erase limits, to reject divisions, to put away all prohibitions, and then ask oneself the question, what has become of knowledge?"

Language matters. "Drugs" are grouped thus for legal purposes, to make them easier to monitor, regulate and control. The spectrum of moral panics and culture wars fabricated around recreational drug use are rooted in neoliberalism, racism and attempts to control "subordinated groups perceived to pose a threat to the order of the body politic".[61] At the rave, drugs are freely given and shared among friends and lovers in pursuit of parallel journeys through the folds of time and space. And capitalist scarcity is liquified in druggy queer abundance and temporality, as a sniff of poppers creates intergenerational bonds between all the queers who have taken a hit and all those who will.

On a more literal level, the party is a place where we can make things happen; where we can mobilise people through the simple act of providing them with a reason to gather. As AIDS ravaged its way through the community, broad coalitions formed between gays and lesbians and trans people, sex workers and unhoused women – all abandoned by formal structures of care. And the party quickly developed into something more – a form of joyful resistance in the face of unfathomable pain. As journalist and author Steve Weinstein, who has been covering the AIDS crisis since the early '80s, shared in 2015: "As so often happens in times of overwhelming calamity, we sought escape…in the flashing lights, blaring sound and packed dance floors of nightclubs and Circuit party weekends."[62] It was here, in this sensory womb, that the community filled their cups so that they once again could pour into caretaking and mutual aid. Not only as "escapist fantasylands", but also as health clinics, information centres and activist meeting grounds.[63]

"Drag queens would hand out safe sex kits with condoms, lube, and hotline numbers…Posters for street actions would be up at the club door, and there was always a big bowl of condoms at the bar. There would often be tables with safe sex information or people handing out ACT UP and Queer Nation stickers and buttons," photographer Melissa Hawkins told *Them*. "There was a real sense of community in the face of the epidemic, even though people had their differences. It was a vital social network for getting information out there."

Pawan tells me that the Kolkatan queer community also organised parties as hubs for education, mobilisation and fundraising in the late '90s and early '00s. To celebrate the end of the 1999 Network East conference – a biennial gathering of queer folks from across Eastern and Northeastern India held in Kolkata – Counsel Club hosted its first paid party on New Years' Eve to raise funds for their support network. And, in 2001, they held a fashion show at a rented wedding house in the Park Circus neighbourhood with a theme of "gay and green" to honour queer people's connection to nature – both in the physical sense of parks providing meeting and cruising spots, and in a more ephemeral sense of queerness as a naturally-occurring expression.

Of course, parties with a purpose are not a novel concept. Recognition and homage must be paid to the Kenyan tradition of harambee, meaning "all pull together" in Kiswahili, Black Americans' rent parties originating in 1920s Harlem, kitty parties hosted by women in post-partition India, and many other examples in the histories of socio-politically marginalised communities. But in combination with the deep meaning the club holds for the queers, there's something particularly powerful in our desire and ability to use what is often demonised as a "debauched" aspect of gay culture to drive profound and meaningful change. To reclaim the night as a period of potent possibility outside of conventional time and create access to what has been historically kept from us – education, multi-generational kinship and financial support.

Today, a potent subculture often operating on the margins, the global queer club community carries on the tradition of nightlife as tangible resistance to mobilise around inequality, oppression and humanitarian crises. As the Oramics collective – a platform created to empower women, non-binary and queer people in the Polish electronic music scene – sells fundraising records to support queers impacted by the anti-LGBT zones; an all-trans art collective The Pansy Collective delivers disaster relief to those impacted by Hurricane Helene in North Carolina. In 2024, Amsterdam-based Ravers for Palestine also partnered with London's Queers for Palestine on a Strike Fund to support artists withdrawing their labour from cultural institutions in solidarity with Palestine. These hubs of solidarity lay the foundations for the world we fight to create. They connect the present reality to the imagined futurity.

For the dancefloor is *not* utopia. Not in the UK or in India, or in Uganda or Australia – not anywhere touched by white supremacy, colonialism and extractionism.

Not for everyone, anyway. Not automatically. Not for me. Not for Black, Brown and Indigenous queers – or for other racialized communities. Not for femmes; for butch dykes; or sissy twinks. Not for fat bodies. Not for those who challenge white ideals of beauty. Nor for disabled folk. Often not for the working-class or the sober partiers. Not for gender non-conformers or trans people, and especially not for Black trans women.

Important as they are in our history and cultural memory, the clubs and circuit parties of the late 1900s United States did not offer the same refuge even for all gay cis men, let alone the diverse queer community. Although "a debauched Hollywood pleasure palace", the infamous Studio One came under fire when, in 1975, the *Los Angeles Free Press* reported that people of colour were frequently denied entrance.[64] When the owner, Scott Forbes, was quizzed on this policy, his response dripped with classism and racism as he explained that "if you're not dressed properly, if you smell bad, you don't get in."[65]

In 2016, Jeremy Joseph, owner of the long-running London club G-A-Y, blamed a rise in crime on "Somalians", resolving to "claim Soho back".[66] Theatron, one of the largest gay clubs in Latin America, faced protests in 2021 after years of discriminatory door policies, with staff misgendering trans women and turning away gender non-conforming folk who weren't "cis-passing".[67] In 2023, world-famous Berlin club Berghain – which is still predominantly gay and positions itself as a leader of counterculture – came under criticism for deplatforming pro-Palestinian artists.[68] And disabled queers often note the lack of accessibility of queer venues and events, flagging that their participation in this core cultural activity is treated as an inconvenience or afterthought.[69]

The party does not automatically prefigure utopia because everyone who attends shares a non-normative sexual desire or presentation. Perhaps we now consider the words of Michael Warner through a more critical lens. Is rejection from "a world of norms" precedent enough for communality, or does this ignore the impact of intersectionality and excuse queer individuals of their own unconscious biases? Unless the spaces where we gather, the *constructed situations* within which we party, actively create boundaries that subvert and dismantle oppressive structures, can they consciously model the futures we dare to dream – grounding their hedonism in collective care and liberation – and hold ravers in both love and accountability?

Ultimately, if you can't imagine it – if you can't see it – then it's harder to realise. This is where we look to temporary and transient parties and "club nights", which often exist on the down-low, resist legitimisation and centre the sounds of counterculture and experimentation.

These codified nomadic events act as heterotopic hubs that subvert the power dynamics of mainstream society to centre the needs, interests and desires of those most marginalised.[70]

Just as "circuit parties" provided escape and education for (mostly) cis white gay men, alternate spaces for Black lesbians, queer punks and gender non-conforming folk popped up in parallel. Ghaziani writes about private "rent parties" thrown by Black lesbians in postwar Detroit – both to offer a safer space than the bars occupied by prejudiced white women and to help cover the high rents of Harlem apartments.[71] I also think fondly of Club Kali, a London-based club-night centring South Asian queers, founded in 1995 by DJ Ritu MBE and Rita. Of The Stud, a Los-Angeles punk bar of the 1970s-'80s. And of nights out for transfeminine folk at Manchester's Rembrandt in the 1980s, organised by Northern Concord.

"No 'queer utopias' for me, please. I wanna see a real mission statement about what we are trying to get done with the music we are putting forward," states London-based DJ Karlie Marx.

Karlie is the founder of several such club nights, including PLASTYK, which aims to unite different communities of lesbians and "centre the music and experiences of trans femme lesbians who have been left out of mainstream lesbian culture". Through a clear vision rooted in understanding sociopolitical shortcomings, Karlie's nights serve the tangible needs of the community, while subverting power dynamics and modelling a futuristic togetherness. And they do this while loudly honouring the unparalleled contribution of Black culture and artists to dance music.

"That for me is also how you throw a good party," Karlie continues. "You follow the thread of what you wanna achieve socially or politically and you let that guide the music. And vice versa."

Rather than "enforcing" certain values, which speaks to a policing of experience, organisers create intentional environments through guidelines, cooldown spaces and designated playrooms, and trained welfare staff that provide a cosier alternative to the intimidating-bouncer-with-a-torch trope. Bussy Temple in Singapore foster a safer space through invite-only gatherings where "queer kin would invite other queer kin and join for a night of thrashing".[72] And London-based Riposte – a queer "art rave" and a personal favourite – often open their parties with grounding welcome rituals. They also curate diverse line-ups, sometimes using an open-call system for transparency and to provide opportunities for those less experienced. Thus creating a more liberatory space that welcomes you into the night, pulsating with new connections and somewhat freed from the anxiety of the unknown, uncomfortable and uncontrollable.

Raves align with conceptualisations of the 4Ds in human rituals that generate altered states of consciousness and build world-making bonds: dance, drums, sleep deprivation, and drugs.[73] Thus, it's unsurprising that without drugs, sober ravers are still able to experience much togetherness, transformation and ecstatic temporality – perhaps even with more presence, especially if they're in recovery. In response to the prevalence of substance abuse in the queer community, a growing range of queer nightlife is centring a sober experience. In Chicago, themed warehouse party In Bed By Ten celebrates Chicago house music; in Berlin, Lemonade Queers host parties with a connection space, games and a variety show; and in London, Misery Party – a grassroots mental health collective – centres radical healing for queer, trans and intersex people of colour through plant medicine workshops and parties that serve food, host workshops and centre artistry.

These events are in themselves disruptive and responsive heterotopias that subvert unspoken rules of a rave. Rather than automatically replicating habits or structures that can lead to harm – and thus contradict the ethos of queer hedonism – they renew the party by creating these same utopian worlds through alternate *hedono-futuristic* avenues, such as shared nourishment, creativity and play.

They affirm that the dancefloor *is* refuge; the dancefloor *is* resistance; and we have the power to transform the dancefloor into anything we want, or need, it to be.

Chapter 3
Paidia//Expression

paidia. *Borrowed from Ancient Greek* παιδιά *(paidiá, "childish play, amusement"), from* παῖς *(paîs, "child"). Greek goddess of play and jest. Puppy love, flirtation; playful and silly.*

In 1971, the inaugural meeting of the Nationwide Festival of Light – an Evangelical Christian event "promoting traditional family values" by opposing homosexuality, abortion rights and sex work – was disrupted by a group of radical drag queens.[74] Some dressed as nuns did the conga down the aisle of the Methodist Central Hall in Westminster, lifting up their skirts and making obscene gestures, while others released mice amongst the attendees' skirts and flagrantly kissed their same-sex partners.[75] While a side group snuck into the basement to pull the plugs and plunge the hall into darkness, drag artists in wigs, pearls and fishnets slow-clapped to break the stunned silence.

Shock, humour and general fuckery are deeply embedded in the way queer people have expressed their anger and protested. Through sudden, loud, brief actions that combined protest with performance art – called "zaps" – gay rights activists in the '70s confronted discrimination directly and garnered media attention for their cause. Led by the actions of Gay Activists Alliance, playful zap tactics included interrupting live broadcasts, provocative dress-up and pieing anti-gay rights campaigners in the face. AIDS activists also adopted a comic frame to repaint the crisis in human terms, build community and garner public attention when nobody would give them any. As Rachel Pepper, an early Queer Nation member, told KQED in 2019: "…when you are in the midst of a crisis and an epidemic you also have to laugh, and you have to find humour, and you have to love, and you have to live intensely every day, because you don't know if you're going to be alive in a year."[76]

Members of grassroots AIDS activist group ACT UP (AIDS Coalition to Unleash Power) staged die-ins across the United States – with protestors holding tombstone-shaped placards that said "RIP KILLED BY THE F.D.A." outside the Food and Drug Administration in Maryland. Other groups published gallows humour zines, such as *Infected Faggot Perspectives* and *Diseased*

Pariah News, which provided "a forum for infected people to share their thoughts, feelings, art, writing, and brownie recipes in an atmosphere free of teddy bears, magic rocks, and seronegative guilt."[77] In 1984 when solidarity group Lesbians and Gays Support the Miners were dubbed "perverts" in *The Sun*, they responded by hosting "Pits & Perverts" – a massive fundraising event at the Electric Ballroom in Camden – raising the equivalent of more than £20,000 today – for the striking miners as then-Prime Minister Margaret Thatcher decimated the predominantly working class mining industry.[78]

As LGSM organiser Mark Ashton states in *Pride,* the 2014 film about the group's activities: "When somebody calls you a name...You take it and own it." At its crux, this queer tradition playfully subverts conventional power dynamics. When the gays loudly call each other "fags" and lesbians wear leather jackets with "DYKE" emblazoned across the back, we stick our middle finger up at society with a sneer and cheeky wink as if to say: "We're here and we're queer and we're proud – what're you gonna do about it?"

It's the pleasure derived from this "play" – the love of holding, stretching and morphing the edges of reality as if it were brightly coloured dough – that is *paidia* (not to be confused with *paideia*, from ancient Greek, meaning "education" or "learning"). Although "play" for the Ancient Greeks included a range of activities, from dancing and singing to more "serious business", such as sport and drama[79] – *paidia* was a feeling first, of joy and delight, that inspired people to express their pleasure through play.[80] It was this playful desire that may have urged Alcibiades to challenge Socrates to a wrestling match as a means of seduction in Plato's *Symposium*, the fantasy of their oiled entangled bodies tugging on the classical links between play and erotic pleasure. Indeed so intertwined that a common word for flirting was *paizein* or *sumpaizein*, meaning "to play" or "play together". Yet, it's here that we truly begin to expand our understanding of hedonism beyond experiences commonly associated with the term, such as sex, clubbing and drugs. Although there isn't much evidence that the Greeks conceived of such an abstract notion of play, for Plato, *paidia* did belong in its own overarching category, which included art that does not merely reflect or mirror the real world, but rather plays with artistic objects – challenging, distorting and subverting reality to create prefigurative heterotopias on canvas or stage.

Such is the case with the radical drag, which – although building on a long history of female impersonation – intends more actively to upset societal norms along with protesting the objectification and fetishisation of womanhood. It can involve the donning of "women's clothing" by gay men without "falsies; or pretence, or parodying women" to confuse "sex and gender rules as laid down by compulsory heterosexuality".[81] It also can look like the rejection of any gendered, or even human, appearance through the creation of fantastical creatures, dismantling the concept of binary gender and allowing us to imagine the existence of the "other". It especially allows trans and gender nonconforming artists not only to invent and express themselves, but also to create a more creative, witty and beautiful world. For example, radical drag as practiced by late '60s-early '70s visionary avante-garde hippie theatre group The Cockettes – which would go on to inspire David Bowie, The Rocky Horror Picture Show and designer Marc Jacobs – was "a sort of shock therapy cabaret with blatant homosexuality, transexuality, gender fuck, foul language, nudity, and high drag".[82] Featuring glittery beards, exaggerated makeup and costumes that combined surrealism with old Hollywood, their drag played with the boundaries of palatability, and beauty. It was sensational; it was confronting. It was camp.

The history of drag as we know it is rooted in the dismantling of hegemonic expectations and a sharing in play and pleasure. At a time when the drag scene was monopolised by white men and white beauty standards – and people of colour who participated were told to whiten their faces – Black queens in 1960s Harlem threw their own competitions and performances. Here, the Black and later Latinx queer communities made ballroom an "underground sensation" that "refused the power of mainstream representation",[83] creating parallels worlds where mainstream beauty standards were subverted and looks instead shaped around the bodies and features of more marginalised groups. Through the ritual of balls, of the long process of putting on and taking off elaborate looks, and of stylised performance, queens still find community, safety and joy in times and places where they're under threat. In 2024, the Haus of Andeti hosted perhaps Kenya's only known kiki – a less formal ball taking its name from the raucous hangs of queer friendship groups – as a balm during a sociopolitically volatile time for Kenya.[84] The theme of Denim on Denim allowed for playful interpretations of an accessible fabric, as the informal structure created room for figuring-it-out. In a country where same-sex relationships are illegal and carry a maximum of 14 years' imprisonment, drag holds a cunty key to safer and more joyful futures.

Indeed, the queer culture of "Camp" itself creates codified heterotopias of pleasure and fuckery. Regardless of whether campness as a stylised view of the world can be political in the way that drag as an artform is to its core – and writer Susan Sontag's *Notes on 'Camp'* dictate not, perhaps because to *intend* to be campy is often less satisfying and sometimes harmful[85] – its queer eye lends itself to a bastardisation of the normative and a reclamation of the "too much". Thus, it's partly the campness within the queer low culture of radical drag and performance art that, combined with socio-political themes and contexts, allows it to deliver disruptive and powerful messages packaged up in all that is playful and anti-serious. Drag bubbles the aspect of Camp that perceives Beings-as-Playing-a-Role – that highlights the constructs of normativity, of gender as a performance – to the surface for all to see.

The costumes and make-up adopted as part of such drag also play a key role in its ability to interrupt and innovate. Indeed, camp taste lashes adoration both on the practice of going against the grain of one's binary gendered expectations and of mocking those very traits through exaggeration. From androgynous looks to high femme and butch-camp, the history and culture of queer fashion has long challenged the limitations of hegemony. Thus it was for the Roots Lesbians in '80s Britain, who combined aspects of Black or Asian traditional garments with lesbian fashion to wear their heritage with pride in a racially hostile environment. Also for the butch dykes that embrace their terribleness – their "ugliness" in the eyes of the patriarchy – to disrupt conventional ideals of feminine beauty.[86] And so it is for the punk tomboy who "defies conventional gender paradigms" showcasing "a clear effort to remake childhood gender" through style that rejects "natural femininity".[87]

In exploring the tomboy as a separate – and more actively gender-rejecting – phenomenon than androgyny in his essay *Oh Bondoge, Up Yours!*, queer academic Jack

Halberstam highlights how "subcultural forms like punk and riot grrl have generated queer girls, often queer tomboys with queer futures". There also is a queer temporality at play with the punk tomboy – a rejection of the inevitability of adult femininity and conventional "womanhood" – that allows for the manifestation of alternate futures. And a celebration of the changemaking power of rage and rebellion traditionally kept from those socialised as girls. He gives one example of iconic punk pioneer Poly Styrene – frontwoman of late-'70s punk rock band X-Ray Spex – with her dayglo clothes, heavy braces and songs that demanded "liberation from the bondage of gender and consumerism". I also think of The Slits, perhaps one of the most influential all-female punk rock bands of the '70s, with their tousled greasy hair and reimagined cut-and-paste looks, from a collar-and-tie worn with a sleeveless lycra bodysuit to BDSM harnesses styled with high-femme Pierrot clown costumes.

Just as the multi-faceted hedono-futurism of radical drag aided GLF in making their case loud and proud, queer artists and activists have continued to insert themselves into the narrative with playful and disruptive interventions. For some, it may be a lifeline on an unforgiving road to self-actualisation. In Russia, radical queer performance artist Gene Marvin regularly takes to the streets in otherworldly costumes made of found materials in a silent and stark protest of Putin's invasion of Ukraine and the violence and homophobia of the Russian state – even when faced with police brutality and societal ostracization.[88] Within the divisive landscape of Croatia, writer, film critic and activist Mima Simić leverages bold, high-profile and comedic media appearances to amplify her lesbian experience and combat divisive political demagogy. For others, those most marginalised by the world they live in, it's "a compulsion, a desire, to make their presence known".[89] Often I wonder at the immense talents that pour out of the queer community, especially holding gratitude for the trailblazing artistry of Black women and trans people. From the groundbreaking play-writing of Lorraine Hansberry in the 1950-60s and the healing expansive synthesis of Beverley Glenn-Copeland's pivotal 1986 work *Keyboard Fantasies*, to the 21st century genre-defying and -defining hyperpop soundscapes of the late musician SOPHIE. Indeed, when a people aren't seen or heard, their expression bursts forth with an urgency and an authenticity to cut through the noise.

Queer art forms serve to create a living, breathing archive. In the Prologue to her groundbreaking memoir, *In the Dream House*, author and critic Carmen Maria Machado speaks of the phenomenon of "archival silence".[90] Asking questions around *who* records *what* histories and *why*, she illustrates the "violence of the archive" – spoken of first by Sadiya Hartman on the dearth of contemporaneous African accounts of slavery

– whether enacted through exclusion or deliberate destruction. As such, the archive – the word itself coming from the Greek ἀρχεῖον: *arkheion*, meaning "the house of the ruler" – acts as a hegemonic tool that silences and erases, leaving future generations spiralling into a void of nothingness, forced to reinvent the wheel with no net of recognition to break gently their fall.

Destruction of recorded histories uproots a people through a removal of "representational belonging".[91] For a lack of evidence that we always not only have existed but also thrived makes it harder to believe that we *do* and will *always* continue to do so – and to seek connections where there apparently seem to be none. This form of "symbolic annihilation" is a tactic of oppression by colonial and authoritarian entities, such as the State of Israel, which has destroyed countless ancient monuments, significant places of worship and cultural institutions in its bid to erase the Palestinian existence and will.[92] It's also what took place when the Nazis burned to the ground the library of Jewish homosexual doctor Magnus Hirschfield's *Institut für Sexualwissenschaft* (the Institute for Sexual Research) – containing more than 20,000 rare books, and diagrams and protocols of some of the first evidence of successful male-to-female (MTF) surgical transition.[93] At a time when transgender rights and wellbeing are severely under attack, and the needs of trans youth are being undermined around the world, such a comprehensive historiography of gender non-conforming people could have been transformational.

With a lack of existence of authentic and honest queer stories in official archives, the responsibility falls on us to record our own histories. But as Machado quotes José Esteban Muñoz: "When the historian of queer experience attempts to document a queer past, there is often a gatekeeper, representing a straight present." We often joke about straight historians describing two women who spent their lives together, shared a bed, wrote passionate letters of longing to one another and never married a man as "best friends". And sometimes, the harsh reality of discovery is so fraught with jeopardy that we are pushed to destroy our own records – as journalist Lorena Hickock burned explicit letters between her and First Lady Eleanor Roosevelt. In this context, art perhaps offers a freer playground for symbolic representation and expression of the queer existence and experience. Coded world-making can take place within the constructed realities of paintings, words and theatre, with artistic liberties allowing the inherent queerness to fly under the radar. For example, artists such as Edmund Dulac and Aubrey Beardsley incorporated peacock feathers into their visual art as a secret representation of their sexualities. As visual artist Jamie Crewe said: "Those people had found a vehicle in which to put their desire, to smuggle it into the thing that's existing and already allowed."[94]

Creativity allows us to exist within a transient state between the binary of conceptualisation and realisation; to occupy a space of *what could be* from *what is*. Black feminist political activist and academic Angela Davis spoke of art at the 2018 NYU Skirball Talks as a potential metaphor for a better world that "helps us cultivate the imagination – to make something new of the old", explaining that it "reminds us we are not obligated to recognize what is given simply because it is given". Through storytelling within these constructed situations, we can prefigure worlds constructed upon better ways of living and loving. Through embedding our demands for how we get there in galvanizing and graphic formats, we can create momentum towards achievable goals.

This was realised by Dyke Action Machine (DAM), founded by artist Carrie Moyer and photographer Sue Schaffner as an offshoot from anti-gay violence activist organisation Queer Nation. Plastering the streets of New York City with thousands of posters between 1991 and 2004, they subverted mainstream media and marketing campaigns by "inserting lesbian images into recognizably commercial contexts".[95] This included recasting a 1992 Calvin Klein's advertisement featuring then-publicly-homophobic Mark Wahlberg with lesbians to advocate for dyke visibility. In protest of gay assimilation through military and marriage inclusion, DAM launched the *Lesbian Americans: Don't Sell Out* campaign in 1998, which featured images of dykes against a backdrop of the American flag. By culture jamming via Situationist tactics, they created heterotopic portals that offered "the lesbian viewer all the things she'd been denied by the mainstream: power, inclusion, and the public recognition of identity".[96]

Another group of US-based queer artists also used reclamation and subversion as part of the Silence=Death project founded in 1987. Flipping the pink triangle used by the Nazis to identify prisoners in concentration camps as gay men, they plastered it on posters, t-shirts and placards to protest the silence around the AIDS epidemic. As such, they made something new of the old, and gave that symbol of unspeakable horror a revised meaning. Today, the pink triangle resonates globally as an iconic symbol of queer resilience, collectivity and resistance.

Queer creative play can help create a fictional – but necessary – archive of the marginalised, the absent and the erased. This was the case with activist and cult photographer Del LaGrace Volcano's series *Queer Dyke Cruising* – semi-staged photos of a quartet of lesbians cruising on London's Hamstead Heath. And also with Indian painter Bhupen Khakhar's honest paintings of homosexual desire, which had a significant impact on the Indian cultural scene's understanding and acceptance of queerness. His 1982 painting *Two Men in Benares*, since described as one of his *coming out* paintings, portrays two nude bodies in embrace, their penises laying in parallel against a backdrop of the city of Banares (Varanasi). This canvas washed in yellows, blues and greens embodies utopia, where such touching male intimacy is not ungodly but rather naturally exists alongside activities such as praying and washing in this holy city for Hinduism. First exhibited in 1986 Bombay (Mumbai) to much protest by the Cottage Industries authorities, this work has since been exhibited around the world and broke records at a Sotheby's auction in 2019, fetching equivalent to £200k.[97] Although Khakhar's paintings and sexuality were deligitimised for a decade, he continued to create transgressive work that challenged India's homophobic polity. Within the space of contradiction in a country that both suffers homophobia as a result of the British colonial rule and ascribes homosexuality to morally bankrupt Western influence, his paintings created evidence that gay men simply lived, touched, and ached for warmth all along. They wrote queerness into India's artistic canon.

It also can capture the raw reality in all its complexity. Today, visual artist Zanele Maholi offers another archival fragment through their confronting photographs of the Black LGBTQIA+ community in South Africa, which document their lived experiences to push "a political agenda, using the visuals as means of articulation."[98] Through visual art that – in their own explanation

– allows the subject of queer experience to be felt and understood even by those who don't have the language to grasp its complexities, they shed light on the historical and contemporary discrimination faced by the community. They challenge a society where, despite legal protections for the LGBTQIA+ community in post-apartheid South Africa, the Black queer community in particular continues to experience harassment and violence such as corrective rape: a horrific hate crime in which the victim is raped on the basis of their perceived gender or sexual orientation.

Via projects such as the ongoing Faces and Phases collection – consisting of more than 500 black-and-white portraits of Black lesbian and trans+ people – Maholi centres the authentic expression of their collaborators, holding discussions to ensure each individual has control over how they're portrayed. Although Maholi has made it clear that their work is "not for show or play", it serves as non-mimetic art in that it creates a heterotopia where Black LGBTQIA+ people are centred and honestly represented not as victims but as complex beings, and their voices amplified. There's deep pleasure that can be drawn from this work – from affirmative portraits that are both vulnerable and powerful, from acknowledgement of this duality of our experience – the "mourning and celebrating" – and from records of the tenderness and intimacy of community.

Maholi's collaborative approach to portrait-making also speaks to the cumulative force that queer creativity can foster. Just as dancing together aligns our biophysical systems to foster belonging, research has shown that choir singers' heart-rates synchronise and that musicians playing the same riffs have brain patterns that are virtually identical.[99][100] Indeed, such creative outpourings are clear examples of "various sources of power within the culture of the oppressed that can provide energy for change". As Sontag writes in her essay *Our Culture and the New Sensibility:* "Art today is a new kind of instrument for modifying consciousness and organizing new modes of sensibility".[101] When we come together to strum this instrument, the energy produced can snowball into an unstoppable force for transformation. Take the Singing Revolution, a four-year series of protests that brought hundreds of thousands of Estonians together in a series of mass singing demonstrations between 1987 and 1991, celebrating their unique culture and eventually leading to Estonian independence.

Even the techniques and processes at play contribute to this collectivity. Printmaking, widely used by agitprop art-activists, has been so popular not only due to its accessibility and affordability, but also because it often requires multiple sets of hands. Electronic music challenges and pushes preconceptions and boundaries, creating space for bodies to come together and do the same. And theatre troupes and drag houses have long provided safer havens for queer and trans artists facing unstable housing or rejection from their bio-legal families. "Houses", chosen family collectives led by "mothers" and "fathers", competed at 1960s drag balls – and still offer structure to the drag and ballroom scenes around the world. The Coquettes emerged from KaliFlower, a commune dedicated to distributing free food, and to creating free art and theatre. In 1977 London, the performers of radical drag troupe Bloolips, founded by Bette Bourne, Lavinia Co-op (Vin Fox) and others, occupied and squatted in disused Notting Hill buildings and turned them into drag communes.

During the '70s, queer communes popped up around London, from Notting Hill to Brixton. In the '80s, the Rebel Dykes occupied squats of their own, sharing everything, sometimes with 18 lesbians and a "menagerie of animals" crammed into a 6-person house.[102] These hubs of collective living were "based on a solidarity that [the co-habitants] defined as love"[103] and aligned with calls in the 1971 GLF manifesto for communes that were "a focus of consciousness-raising and of gay liberation activity, a new focal point for members of the gay community."[104] Communality stemming from collaborative art-making challenged gay assimilation in the present, and modelled a pluriversal future through realising its ideal values of commons and collective ethics.

Through seeking pleasure through play – whether for campy enjoyment or political disruption – the queers shared in an ecstatic experience that created space for queer temporality and realised wormholes to utopian futures.

Paidia resulting in, or felt as a result of, authentic expression not only lets us as individuals centre our joy and pleasure, but also fosters connection with others rooted in the sharing and multiplicity of that joy. To enact hedono-futurism is to revel in this pleasure – to bask in the silliness of shock humour, gender fuckery and sexual anarchy. It's to create artistic worlds laden with symbolism, transgression and defiant queer subjectivity. It is to allow this potent source of power to drive us forward in pursuit of liberation for all.

Chapter 4
Agape//Collaboration

agape. *From* Ancient Greek ἀγάπη *(agápē, "love; the love between man and God). A transcendent highest form of love. Manifests in the unselfish, unconditional, sacrificial love between fellow humans.*

The commune, the camp, the community centre. These constructed situations are places where ideas bloom, where connections are fostered, so that we may continue to step out the front door and stand defiant. In the communes of '80s London, the Rebel Dykes, GLF, Bloolips Theatre Group and many other collectives hatched protest plans, created radical art and organised sex parties. They intertwined the personal and the collective, enacting love for friendship and family through collective action, experiencing pleasure rooted in *philia*. As Bloolips co-founder Bette Bourne shared in Stuart Feather's book *Blowing the*

Lid, they'd sometimes reach a "kind of bliss" in the commune, one they hadn't experienced before. It was this that gave them the energy to carry on. "It wasn't drug induced; it was that kind of communal action."

This caretaking through the formation and sustenance of alternate kinship models speaks to love as "an action, a participatory emotion", which bell hooks calls on us to "move beyond the realm of feeling to actualize".[105] The actualization of this love as solidarity and care is *agape*, a kind of entirely unselfish love that is giving, unconditional and sometimes sacrificial. It's a commitment "to nurture our own and other's spiritual growth" in pursuit of shared meaning and purpose, which holds the power to transform pleasure-seeking cultural practice into collaborative liberatory action. The Oxford Dictionary adds an afterthought to its definition of hedonism, stating that "there are various ways of trying to align the pursuit of selfish pleasure with some degree of concern for others". I would go many steps further, and state that hedono-futurism *only* exists where the experience of pleasure is rooted in our concern for others. Where this concern is actualised, not merely felt in passivity.

Here, something metamorphic takes place wherein we, who experience otherness in relation to the world, morph to understand ourselves through the togetherness that we experience with one another. Through the creation of these chosen families, "families formed outside of biological or legal (bio-legal) bonds",[106] we also model a world where interpersonal bonds are formed based on what we *offer* one another, rather than simply who we *are* to one another. Not one that binds us further through transactional or exploitative expectation, but rather one that frees us from prescriptive definitions of "family", "responsibility" and, indeed, "love".

These networks not only re-imagine and transform traditional kinship dynamics but also foster a utopic queer temporality. The "chosen family" creates a queer time and space that exists "in opposition to the institutions of family, heterosexuality, and reproduction", as argued by Jack Halberstam in *In a Queer Time and Place*.[107] It also offers an alternative to the nuclear heteronormative family that promotes traditional gender roles and upholds capitalism by perpetuating inequality, contributing to compartmentalisation of neighbourhoods and communities. As anthropologist Kath Weston outlined in her seminal work, *Families We Choose*, the chosen family is "a refuge specifically generated by and for the queer experience – a core cultural motif that spans generations and borders."[108]

Through providing housing, food, healthcare or transportation in order to "directly engage the social conditions a community seeks to address",[109] intersectional mutual aid networks draw attention to the political landscape that creates need and vulnerability. This, in turn, aids us to organise on both a micro and a macro level, built on an understanding of *what is missing* and *what gaps need filling*. Collective contribution has sustained marginalised communities, such as mixed-status immigrant Latinx families, who create chosen families of migrants to survive the lack and loss of grandparents, aunts, brothers – who may have remained or been forcibly deported by an inhumane immigration system.[110] It also has acted as an adaptive survival strategy for working-class or poor families, and Black and Brown communities – such as those relying on welfare in 1974 urban Midwest.[111]

For queers, the chosen family can be lifesaving. Indeed, it was through these networks that terminally ill gay men living with HIV, ostracised by their bio-legal families, received end-of-life care during the 1980s AIDS crisis. Sociologist Judith Stacey wrote of how lesbians undertook "Herculean levels of caretaking outside default family form". In San Diego, the Women's Caucus of the San Diego Democratic Club formed the *Blood Sisters*, organising blood drives attended by women who "didn't want to have anything to do with men – even gay men".[112] While others volunteered with the anonymous helpline the Lesbian and Gay Switchboard, and organised protest zaps and actions. During an extremely precarious time in gay people's lives – on the precipice of life and death – their primary source of care came through the family they created for themselves. Familial structures in the ballroom scene today still provide African American queer youth with multiple forms of support for HIV prevention.[113]

It was similar networks that enabled the queer community to respond with agility when a new virus emerged in Summer 2022 – disproportionately affecting self-identified gay, bisexual, and other men who have sex with men. Despite being fundamentally different from AIDS – monkeypox was a known virus with existing vaccines – the societal stigma perpetuated by the media, who called it a "gay disease", and medical abandonment by governments rang close to home.[114] Once again, the queers self-organised and got shit done. Community and grassroots organisations disseminated updates, refuted misinformation and signposted vaccination sites. Over the course of the next 6 months, thousands received vaccinations from vans outside queer clubs and sex parties; gay leather conventions handed out condoms, lube and information leaflets; and Grindr collaborated with the Pan American Health Organization to send out alerts, adding a vaccination status field to its interface.

Such rapid response at times of crises is possible partly due to the resilience and collectivity of established collaborative relationships and community spaces, where we "share the power of each other's feelings" – holding one another through grief, joy, rage and euphoric release. Spaces which are largely sustained through the fragments of connection and creativity that fill the spaces in between. The togetherness fostered by these heterotopias creates webs of connection like mycelia between fungi – underground fungal networks – which play a role in the communication of ecosystems and the distribution of resources between plants.[115] Through practicing hedonism rooted in *agape,* we grow these pleasure mycelia. And through daily rituals of care and solidarity practiced alongside one another, we strengthen and sustain them.

The impact of this was evident when Tblisi-based queer techno club Bassiani was raided in 2018 by armed police – who arrested some of its founders along with those of closely-affiliated drug decriminalisation advocacy group White Noise Movement. In response, the two collectives mobilised almost the entire underground community in an afternoon to protest – and dance – outside the Georgian parliament. Over 15,000 queer and allied Georgians brought the rave to the government's doorstep, sustaining their protest through the rejuvenating joy of the very culture they were fighting to preserve. Despite strong opposition from the ruling party, their demand for drug policy reform was successful – in July 2018, the constitutional court legalised cannabis for personal use.[116]

A shining beacon of Georgia's queer nightlife scene, Bassiani is often placed on par with Berghain as a global leader in electronic music innovation. But Bassiani is so much more than a 24-hour den of unthinking hedonism.

Its culture is deeply rooted in political queerness and liberatory action: Horoom Nights – founded in 2016 by activist and music promoter Giorgi Kikonishvilia – calls on ravers to create the spirit of resistance and to "start disobedience by publicly declaring love for each other".[117] According to Georgian queer activist and Bassiani co-collaborator Paata Sabelashvili, "Bassiani isn't a club, it's a social movement to which the music is merely a soundtrack."[118] In fact, the space often acts as a conduit for collective action – an emboldening layover before going face-to-face with Georgia's violent police force. Party-goers are sometimes stamped on entry with the words "Parliament at seven o'clock", "so they know what they have to do as soon as they wake up", while other times projections on the walls countdown the time the ravers have left to sleep before they need to make their way to that evening's protests.

Even in the pre-Bassiani era of the early '00s, it was Georgia's first gay bar Success, founded by Nia Gvatua, that gave the LGBTQIA+ community a place to communicate offline as traditional "family values" took hold when Georgia's economy stabilised in a post-Soviet era. And today – as a host of anti-LGBTQ+ laws are implemented, banning same-sex marriage, gender-affirming care and the depiction of queer people in media – queer clubs, bars and art galleries, such as the Fungus Gallery, serve the role of community centres. The transformational power of this scene is apparent – the organisers who breathe life into the night have visibly changed the way wider society perceives queer people. As Paata told *Attitude*, if you venture to the local Turkish snack bars after a good night out, it's no longer unusual to come across "aggressive macho men downing vodka shots with transsexual women".

This "wood wide web"[119] can act as a metaphor for pluriversal worlds that centre collectivity, reciprocity and oneness with nature, and provide proof that, when we root our joy in shared values, and think of hedonism as a key vein running through the bigger picture in pursuit of liberation, our joy has the potential to transform people and places. Through pleasure-orientated shared experience, these spaces create wormholes to queer futures. Hopelessness is not an innate human condition; it's systemic, enforced consistently to limit the scope of our imaginations, whether through visible violent tactics – such as police brutality – or through austerity. When we create our own heterotopic structures amid it all, we act in opposition to those forces that would have us question the possibility of a better future. Perhaps this is even more the case when these are sites of transience that resist legitimisation and monetisation. When these temporary communities are prepared to dissolve in response to the needs of the occupants – to practice the queer art of failure.

I think of the Greenham Common Women's Peace Camp, where the Rebel Dykes met, and of "Camp

Trans", an annual demonstration and event held outside the trans-exclusionary Michigan Womyn's Music Festival between 1994 and 2015. There now exists an annual festival of the same name, where trans "radicals in communion" embody utopia each summer on a British campsite.[120] In these encampments, protest becomes intertwined with the mundanity of day-to-day life. Rather than an ephemeral event that wrestles to slot into our busy lives, preoccupied with capitalist demands on our capacity, the camp is a home of sorts. In it, we're able to breathe out to fill our lungs with space and time, creating fluid queer temporality through moments of nothing, of boredom. Of stillness and quiet reflection, communed around nourishment and oneness with nature. From shared wild swims, hikes and rest at Camp Trans, to communal meals and community gardens at occupations – this is where the imagination blooms and gathers the potential energy to transform reality.

So it was for the University of Cambridge student encampment, heavily populated by queer organisers who consider all forms of liberation as intertwined – Cambridge for Palestine organiser Gabriela shared with me that "queerness felt unremarkable on the camp, in the most affirming way". Here, they built a garden from donated pallets and broken tents, planting culturally significant flowers and vegetables and educating around Palestinian resistance to ecocide. The abundance cultivated was hedonistic in its revelry in variety, colour, and smell – the garden was a vibrant pocket of resistance amidst the sea of monoculture grass across Cambridge colleges. On those manicured lawns, only senior members and fellows are allowed to walk. But in the camp's community garden, all were welcome to sit, to reflect and to transform the dream of alternate futures into reality, even if just for a while.

This camp was one of many that rose up around the world inspired by the defiant actions of students at Columbia University in April 2024 – who renamed its Hamilton Hall as "Hind's Hall" (in honour of Hind Rajab, a six-year-old Palestinian girl murdered by the Israeli military on 29th January), and responded to intimidation by the administration by writing in big red letters on top of the typed letter, "I AIN'T READING ALL THAT, FREE PALESTINE".[121] From New York and Mexico, to Turkey, India and New Zealand, students pressured their academic institutions to divest from the Israeli state, holding them accountable for their role in upholding apartheid and a genocidal regime. But unlike stories in right-wing and national media that painted these students as the aggressors and the camps as places filled with "hateful language" and "antisemitic agitators" [122] – every scene streamed to my phone from the heart of the encampment painted a picture of a safe, affirming and inspirational community space.

Hubs of collective resistance sustained through a togetherness in pain, grief, joy and release. Worlds within worlds, mini settlements with their own mutual aid networks, open-access medical tents and public art featuring words from Palestinian poets. Over the following months, I watched videos of keffiyeh-wearing students dance Bharatanatyam. I read first-person accounts of grounded atmospheres, where students read books from their camp's liberation library and makeshift choirs sang Black gospel classics. And I spoke to organisers, who found a depth of friendship and a life-long purpose within the cognitive dissonance of the academic university landscape as they stood against an active genocide.

Experiencing hedono-futurism rooted in *agape* can teach us everything about solidarity and about love. Solidarity – which is a manifestation of love as a participatory action creates spaces where we can hold one another and heal from the pain of the present, while practicing and creating better futures. Love rooted in solidarity transcends borders, empowering us to seek pleasure in pursuit of the limitless benefits for a collective over a temporary comfort for the individual. Through accessing healing community spaces via the pleasure mycelia, we create space for others to grow while honouring our own boundaries. And we learn to value each other through radical honesty, accountability and curiosity – beyond socio-political dynamics and interpersonal tensions. As

Gabriela explains: "We often say: I don't like them, but they're my comrades. I love them."

Despite a mutual understanding that everyone wished deeply that the camp wasn't a necessity, their presence was bonded by a shared objective, fostering a depth of meaningful relationality between strangers-turned-comrades-turned-friends. It was this that brought them together for 100 days to share tents, dreams, everything – and to eat dinner together daily, which Gabriela pinpoints as one of the most meaningful aspects of the encampment. Through the ritualistic daily practice of camp-life, with its routines enacted in pursuit of liberation, a better world was embodied within tarp walls. Through the experience of shared pleasure borne of a borderless liberatory love, this world was able to extend across mountains and oceans – at once limitless yet altogether possible.

There's something so magical about food, not only in the way it sustains our living beings but also in the key ceremonial role it plays for countless cultures. Food is an innate connection with ancestral wisdom; and one of the most sincere manifestations of community- and self-care. It can also be deeply playful – with wobbly jellies, throat-numbing spices and vibrant colours – a cornucopia of sensory delights, some even sensual. It can inspire some of the most deep-seated childlike delight and moments of ecstatic bliss. Having grown up in India, I would certainly call the relationship Indians across the nation have with food hedonistic. Hearing family and friends speak of favourite dishes or describe a specific mango devoured last season is poetic and reverent, their words overflowing with an unbearable excitement and adoration. Their eyes closed in contentment and their bodies rolling with pleasure.

There's hedonism in taking the time to feel vegetables between our fingers, to chop with care, to stand over a simmering pot and inhale deep, tasting morsels as we go. And in community, it's an anti-capitalist act to luxuriate together – around the kitchen table – in the tastes and textures rolling over our tongues, letting time slow down and our to-do list dissolve in our mouths. To spend hours discussing and laughing at the inane complexities of our lives, creating bonding memories all tied up in a bow with the über-evocative senses of taste and smell. The sharing of food acts as a tangible model for political collectivity and the power of mutual contribution – "how much more you can have when you grow together", as said by pioneering lesbian activist Karla Jay.[123] What better way to move toward "living in a fundamental way"[124] than by breaking bread with our chosen family and our neighbours to build love and solidarity, in direct opposition to the division sown by hegemonic forces to keep us disparate and, thus, easier to control.

Many of the events that take place at my queer shared home centre food as a point of convergence and non-transactional caretaking. Guests bring homemade dishes to our intimate day parties – affectionately named "Pulse" after both the legume and the beat – and to our annual celebration of the Pagan winter festival, Saturnalia. This potluck tradition sits on the shoulders of our queer elders, especially the dykes. As food writer Reina Gattuso writes, "lesbians have been known to potluck everything from protests to sex parties".[125] She shares how one of the first lesbian organisations in the United States, the Daughters of Bilitis, was founded in 1950s San Francisco by Del Martin and Phyllis Lyon with the sharing of food. The Daughters of Bilitis soon blossomed into chapters across the United States – hosting regular events laden with homemade salads, quiches and cakes where lesbians could flirt, experience affirmation and harness their power for the radical generations to come.

Lesbians would continue to reclaim the undervalued labour of cooking as "woman's work". In 1980, a group of Black lesbian feminists including Audre Lorde and Barbara Smith founded the Kitchen Table: Women of Color Press – a "revolutionary tool" to empower "society's most dispossessed people".[126] In centring the kitchen table, they celebrated the powerful role cooking and sharing food can play in fostering togetherness, starting conversations and inspiring action for change between women – disrupting and disempowering its usage as an oppressive tool of the patriarchy. Across the

Atlantic Ocean, the Rebel Dykes were also feasting at the nodes of their fictive kin networks – engaging with shared meals through the same raunchy, silly and rebellious lens that energised their activism, music-making and BDSM. In the 2021 documentary *Rebel Dykes*, Baya tells of a Christmas attended by 26 friends of friends where, tripping on acid, she took on the task of stuffing and cooking the too-big-for-their-oven turkey. Giggling, she recounts: "I started mixing up apples, onions, breadcrumbs, stuffing. As I was stuffing the turkey, I tripped out… [it was] as if I was in a different galaxy where having sex with a turkey was a perfectly fine thing to do."

Today, LGBTQIA+ action groups continue a long tradition of gathering up the crumbs and converting them into abundance, even in the face of extreme precarity – and of building networks of mutual reliance around shared food. The Outside Project, London's LGBTIQ+ Community Shelter, Centre and Domestic Abuse Refuge, regularly post photos of the communal meals made by their volunteers, staff and service users. In the predominantly white area of Santa Cruz, the Diversity Centre creates a necessary space for queer people of colour to honour and celebrate their ethnic backgrounds with the Queer & Trans People of Color Potluck. And trans chefs cook feasts for 50 at the annual Doll Invasion, a crowd-funded summer takeover of Fire Island aiming to reclaim a now gentrified queer political home.

"I think that chosen family in queer spaces, specifically for queer people of colour, allow for us to love and to be loved in a way that I never could have dreamt of outside of those very specific spaces," anthropologist and community organiser Maiya McQueen tells me about finding community with other queer Black people in San Francisco. "We get to take care of one another, and there isn't any discomfort or any ownership. There's a choice to love even though it's hard sometimes."

Although originally hypothesised in the context of heterosexual romantic relationships, Simone de Beauvoir's understanding of "authentic love" comes to mind.[127] For de Beauvoir, this form of love – in contrast to "inauthentic love" – is a love that is non-possessive and non-submissive. It both acknowledges our differences and considers us as equals in relationality. It's a love that not only recognises, respects and embodies our own eroticism, but holds up a mirror to the other to affirm and share in theirs, too. Solidarity as authentic love is revolutionary; it shows us that we can love strangers and experience a reciprocity. It makes room for our shared imagination to transcend the foreclosure of possibility as imposed upon us by hegemonic bodies. And it provides a safety net, a trampoline from which to launch, imbuing us with the energy to be more audacious. To take more risks, to imagine unfettered worlds, and to act more boldly to create them.

Indeed, when I look around our safe haven in North London, it's not the living room curtains made of recycled DVDs, the sculptures of candle wax that adorn countless recycled wine bottles or the nude BDSM-orientated art peppering the walls that stands out to me as a signifier of the deep-rooted trans love that flows through its hallways – although, yes, all those things are undoubtedly queer as all hell. It's the early morning birthday breakfasts held without fail for each of the seven occupants, the resources unearthed in a heartbeat when one of us is caught off guard by a transphobic colleague and the meals shared in times of sickness. It's the tears that flow freely and are held with grace, the uncontrollable giggles from deep within our bellies and all the things that are understood without having to be said. Through shared euphoria at parties and raves, long winding dinners and collaborative paintings on giant canvases, we've built, strengthened and maintained kinship bonds rooted in pleasure which hold us afloat in sun-soaked waters that are – sometimes – thicker than the blood flowing through our veins. And allow us to adventure far and wide, steered by our will to create a better world – with the knowledge that, when we need to rest, rage or lick our wounds, we will be held with gentle joy and love in our own little utopia.

Conclusion
Pragma

pragma. *From the Ancient Greek root πρᾶγμα (prâgma, "a thing done, a fact"). A matured, compassionate and enduring love. This love requires patience and compromise from all parties involved, and a commitment to staying in love, not simply falling in love.*

Speckled sunbeams shining through smoke-filled canopies, a world tinted momentarily pink and heavy with the familiar scent of protest. Pride flags waving in time to queer anthems, bathed in disco fireflies – reflections off sequined ballgowns and leather armour. Witty placards and bright pink banners, spray-painted, smudged, scrawled, embroidered: "OUR KIDS WILL HAVE TRANS PARENTS". The repetitive hum of the drums, the rousing rally of the hoots and the cheers. And the love, oh so much love. Hands held, cheeks kissed, videos posed-for, cigarettes smoked, snacks passed from hand-to-mouth – as the air fills with echoing chants: "Whose streets? Our streets!"

This, to me, is hedonism. This collective action that is rooted in authentic love, in *agape*, that empowers us to demand better for our communities and to enact solidarity with others. Our Pride will always be a protest first, whether embodied in the dungeon, on the dancefloor, on the canvas, or in the streets – but that doesn't mean it can't be saturated with pleasure in all its forms. Because loving, celebrating and enjoying ourselves comes with the knowledge that we deserve better. We deserve our lives to be held in higher regard. We deserve to dream, to build and to flourish with freedom and safety. We deserve liberation from oppressive hegemonic forces – not only for ourselves, but for everyone.

The ruling class would prefer us to be contained/containable, to remain boxed up and categorizable. To limit both the expansive potentials of our physical selves and the horizons of our imaginations. To let the heavy walls close in on us – seemingly impossible to push back – and for the smallness to wear us down. To ultimately give up the fight due to exhaustion and despair. But through hedono-futurism, we can know that we don't need to fight their fight with the master's tools[128] – we can find another way. We can take up the space historically and systematically denied to us. We can let our pleasure be the guiding light – as seen on a banner from the first Pride in London march in 1972 – "out of the closet and into the streets".

Cruising has always been about taking up space, about marginalised peoples staking a claim to the world around them. As artefacts of this ritual of brief encounter litter public places from the Midwest to the Indian Ocean, they memorialise the queer ability to transform both space and self through hedonism. This metamorphosis also takes place through DIY club nights, pop-up lesbian bars and BDSM dungeons, where we create shared heterotopias that resist the commodification of eroticism. When we transform our faces and bodies to occupy campy realms of alternate innovation – in flamboyance, monstrosity and punk resistance – we take up a visual and symbolic space that is withheld by binary gendered expectations and normativity. We insert ourselves into the narrative, inflating our lungs to fill the metropolis, the cultural institute and the media outlet, when we ad-hack, create protest street art and express our creativity in all its weird and wonderful ways. And, through community, mutual aid and protest, we reclaim privatised care and land in reconnection with nature – filling empty buildings with our chosen families, campsites with moments of stillness and the streets with our demands.

Taking up this space to create untested alternate worlds is not an easy task. Everywhere we look, public access to cities is being ripped apart by developments and stability is increasingly difficult to afford; it's no surprise that our right – and confidence – to roam, linger and lounge feels shoved in a corner and forgotten. As the heavy hand of capitalism tightens its fist around our barely surviving necks, hustle culture seeps in all the gaps and distorts the romance and transformational potential of failure into something undesirable. We can't afford to pay our bills; the weekly shop has doubled in price; we don't have the time to call our grandparents. Convenience is king. Indeed, the instant gratification of apps like Grindr and Tinder sings a siren song amongst a sea of detachment. There's less chance of a let-down; no walking home alone after "time wasted" exchanging small talk in a bar or waiting around in a filthy toilet. Why would we support a grassroots club night that's still figuring out its sound when it's much easier to tag along to the mega-club, especially if it looks good on our social media? Sometimes, *showing up* through donating money, food or our time – or sacrificing personal comfort to occupy and protest – just doesn't seem doable (or worth it, because why would we even bother if change feels impossible?).

Hedono-futurism not only shows us that pluriversal futures are possible, but also directly challenges "the tyranny of convenience", as outlined by legal scholar Tim Wu in his 2018 essay.[129] Although presented to us as a route to liberation, convenience culture – especially in the ways modern technology has commodified individualism and connection – instead can become a "constraint on what we are willing to do, and thus in a subtle way it can enslave us." When we let convenience be our priority, over our other values, we become more susceptible to the whims of those who have the power and want to keep it. We give away the key to our freedoms in the name of superficial ease. We let governments and corporations constrict the fullness and complexities of our identities, relationships and imaginations.

Ultimately, our convenience also often comes at the cost of someone else. When we use AI to undertake research or write our essays, we let its learned and coded biases – whether racist, misogynistic or countless other prejudices – more blatantly dictate our conclusions. When we shop on Amazon, buy fast fashion or automatically choose a short-haul flight over a longer train journey, we play a role in oppression of working-class and Global South communities, and the destruction of our planet. When we buy a Coca-Cola or a SodaStream, even though we *know* (in theory) the power of economic boycotts in driving change, we give a free pass to colonial genocidal regimes. But, when our own day-to-day lives can seem so unmanageable, how do we resist buying into the "cult of convenience" – the siren call of "whatever I want, whenever and however I want it"?

We can resist it through activating, strengthening and enjoying the pleasure mycelia. Rather than buying into self-care that requires us to buy infinite products, when we choose instead to experience joy, rest and healing in community, we build the relationships that help us pick connection and liberation over convenience and conformity – that lighten the load so that we may choose our own adventure. Your friend may cook dinner so that you don't have to grab a McDonald's, or know someone who has a spare bed so you don't have to use AirBnb. You might be able to borrow that sound system for your party rather than ordering it for next-day delivery. A DIY dyke might just pop round and fix your chest of drawers – so you can instead donate to a trans person's healthcare fundraiser. Or you might be able to access a community mutual aid fund yourself to help pay rent – freeing up your Saturday to pick up a placard instead of another bar shift. Through these pathways, pleasure-rooted activities that are *inconvenient* build anti-capitalist, radical and revolutionary foundations. As Wu writes: "Sometimes struggle is a solution."

Taking the seemingly inconvenient route where we don't have to compromise our other values can be rewarding precisely because we learn how to resist in small – but meaningful – ways. Through daily practice, we begin to embed this resistance into our persons, communities and futures. Political activist and scholar Angela Davis famously said during a 2014 lecture at Southern Illinois University: "You have to act as if it were possible to radically transform the world. And you have to do it all the time." Hedono-futurism rooted in the breadth of pleasure and love helps us do this all the time. Because it not only empowers us to take up space, but also guides us in understanding how *much* space to take up. When to stop looking for the next best thing – the bigger high, the better sexual experience, the hotter afters to crash. It helps us answer when to centre our voices and experiences and when to step back – and if we should be taking up the most room on the dancefloor. It helps us learn from the mistakes of our elders so that we can build solidarity across communities and movements. And to respect boycotts – seeing the role that queer nightlife plays in the pinkwashing of violent colonial bodies – even at the expense of a really good night out.[130]

Things feel genuinely scary right now. President Trump of the United States and his billionaire friends are inflicting their hateful and divisive agenda on the most marginalised – removing mentions of intersex and trans people from governmental websites,[131] halting gender-affirming healthcare for trans youth[132] and changing trans people's gender markers on official documents without their consent.[133] Hindutva is sowing hatred and driving mass violence against Muslims in India, and limiting their rights; the Hungarian Orbán government has implemented a whole host of anti-LGBTQ+ laws since 2020; the UK's anti-immigration policy is inhumane, with the

Home Office regularly conducting deportation raids; and every year seems to break records as the hottest year to date, as coral reefs die while fossil fuel companies get rich. We're overwhelmed, overstimulated and in paralysis. We're absorbing more information via social media than we're evolved to process in real-time – switching between 2-minute hacks, celebrity faux pas and live-streamed genocides. We need each other now, perhaps more than ever.

As a community with a shorter actual or perceived life expectancy than our cis-heterosexual counterparts, it's little surprise that we tend to live moment-to-moment.[134][135] A generation of queer elders was taken from us by a negligent and biased society – we still carry within us the memory of losing everyone we loved. But it's through togetherness that we can address our individual and intergenerational trauma. We're social animals, evolved to comfort one another and to heal in relation with others.[136] In opposition to societally-ingrained individualism, we actually need community to break out of bystander paralysis[137] and to "act as if it were possible to radically transform the world". In opposition to binary "dump him" and "cancel" culture, we need to repair social rupture and grow together with accountability. It's through practicing hedono-futurism rooted in care and solidarity that we can come to believe not only that a better future is possible, but that we'll live long enough to see it.

Writing on our defence against the rise of fascism, McKenzie Wark proposed that our vision for "the good life" is to be "found in fragments of the everyday when we live without dead time… When we glimpse another city for another life."[138] These are the heterotopias we model when we're fucking, dancing, painting, feeding our friends, setting up camp in protest. These are the sites where we create longevity for our communities through practicing love as action over and over again – through *pragma*. Where we embody and realise the creation of queer pluriversal utopias.

References

1. Foucault, M. (1984) 'Of Other Spaces: Utopias and Heterotopias', Architecture /Mouvement/ Continuité, no. 5, pp. 46-49.
2. Goldman, E. (1969) Anarchism and Other Essays. 3rd. NY: Dover Publications Inc.
3. *Pluriverse: A Post-Development Dictionary* (2019). Edited by Kothari A., Salleh A., Escobar A., Demaria F. and Acosta A. India: Tulika Books.
4. Blackburn, S. (2008). 'hedonism' in *The Oxford Dictionary of Philosophy*. Second edition. [Online]. UK: Oxford University Press. Available from: https://www.oxfordreference.com/display/10.1093/acref/9780199541430.001.0001/acref-9780199541430. (Last accessed: 11 March 2025).
5. McIntosh, C. (2013). 'hedonism' in *Cambridge Advanced Learner's Dictionary & Thesaurus*. Fourth edition. [Online]. UK: Cambridge University Press. Available from: https://dictionary.cambridge.org/dictionary/english/hedonism. (Last accessed: 11 March 2025).
6. The Editors of Encyclopaedia Britannica (2025). 'hedonism' in *Encyclopaedia Britannica*. [Online]. Available from: https://www.britannica.com/topic/hedonism. (Last accessed: 11 March 2025).
7. Beta, A. (2015). 'Electronic Warfare: The Political Legacy of Detroit Techno'. *Pitchfork*, (January). [Online] Available at: https://pitchfork.com/features/electric-fling/9588-electronic-warfare-the-political-legacy-of-detroit-techno/. (Last accessed: 11 March 2025).
8. Mishan, L. (2020). 'Today's Chefs are Honoring a Vital Tradition: Feeding the Revolution'. *NY Times*, (August). [Online]

    Available at: https://www.nytimes.com/2020/08/28/t-magazine/food-protest-revolution.html. (Last accessed: 11 March 2025).

9   Al Jazeera (2024). *Dabke dance troupe brings relief to Gaza's war-weary children*. Available at: https://www.aljazeera.com/program/newsfeed/2024/5/28/dabke-dance-troupe-brings-relief-to-gazas-war-weary-children. (Last accessed: 11 March 2025).

10   Lorde, A. (1984). 'Uses of the Erotic: The Erotic as Power', in Lorde, A. *Sister Outsider: Essays and Speeches*. CA: The Crossing Press, pp. 53-55.

11   Parlett, J. (2019). 'The Complex Queer Literary History of Fire Island', *Literary Hub*, (June). [Online] Available at: https://lithub.com/the-complex-queer-literary-history-of-fire-island/. (Last accessed: 11 March 2025).

12   Winston, J. (2021). *Greedy: Notes From a Bisexual Who Wants Too Much*. NY: Simon & Schuster.

13   Washington B. and Vuong, O. (2020). 'All The Ways To Be with Bryan Washington & Ocean Vuong', *The A24 Podcast*. [Podcast] Available at: https://a24films.com/notes/2020/12/all-the-ways-to-be-with-bryan-washington-ocean-vuong. (Last accessed: 11 March 2025).

14   Mitchell, L. (1977). *The Faggots & Their Friends Between Revolutions*. Third edition. NY: Nightboat Books, p. 36.

15   Moseley, A. 'Philosophy of Love', in *The Internet Encyclopedia of Philosophy*. [Online]. Available from: https://iep.utm.edu/love/. (Last accessed: 11 March 2025).

16   Frost, N. (2017). 'How the 18th-Century Gay Bar Survived and Thrived in a Deadly Environment', *Atlas Obscura*, (December). Available at: https://www.atlasobscura.com/articles/regency-gay-bar-molly-houses. (Last accessed: 11 March 2025).

17   Michael, G. (2007). 'George Talks: His Frankest Interview Ever'. Interviewed by Smith, R and Pafford, S. *Gay Times*, (July). Available at: https://gmforever.com/george-michaels-interview-with-gay-times-2007/. (Last accessed: 11 March 2025).

18   Espinoza, A. (2019). *Cruising: An Intimate History of a Radical Pastime*. LA: Unnamed Press, p. 63.

19   Mitchell, L. (1977). *The Faggots & Their Friends Between Revolutions*. Third edition. NY: Nightboat Books, p. 17.
20   Halberstam, J. (2011). *The Queer Art of Failure*. NC, United States: Duke University Press, p. 121.
21   Espinoza, A. (2019). *Cruising: An Intimate History of a Radical Pastime*. LA: Unnamed Press, pp. 78, 83, 84.
22   The Saint Foundation (2019). *The Handkerchief Code, According to 'Bob Damron's Address Book' in 1980*. Available at: https://www.thesaintfoundation.org/community/hanky-code-bob-damrons-address-book. (Last accessed: 11 March 2025).
23   Gander, K. (2018). 'Public toilets and private affairs: Why the history of gay cruising deserves an exhibition', *International Business Times*, (January). Available at: https://www.ibtimes.co.uk/public-toilets-private-affairs-why-history-gay-cruising-deserves-exhibition-1654243. (Last accessed: 11 March 2025).
24   Espinoza, A. (2019). *Cruising: An Intimate History of a Radical Pastime*. LA: Unnamed Press, p. 60.
25   Atherton Lin, J. (2021). *Gay Bar: Why We Went Out*. UK: Granta Publications, p. 28.
26   0-60_now_what (2023). *Euphoria is being cruised by gay men!* [Reddit]. Available at: https://www.reddit.com/r/FTMOver30/comments/16koy7n/euphoria_is_being_cruised_by_gay_men/. (Last accessed: 11 March 2025).
27   Espinoza, A. (2019). *Cruising: An Intimate History of a Radical Pastime*. LA: Unnamed Press, p. 55.
28   DarkerScorp (2023). *Gay Dating in Russia*. [Reddit]. Available at: https://www.reddit.com/r/AskARussian/comments/zuj2hj/gay_dating_in_russia/. (Last accessed: 11 March 2025).
29   Human Rights Watch (2019). *Russia: New Anti-Gay Crackdown in Chechnya*. Available at: https://www.hrw.org/news/2019/05/08/russia-new-anti-gay-crackdown-chechnya. (Last accessed: 11 March 2025).
30   Espinoza, A. (2019). *Cruising: An Intimate History of a Radical Pastime*. LA: Unnamed Press, p. 184.
31   Leavell, J. (2017). 'The Freedom and Beauty I Found Cruising for Sex', *VICE Magazine*, (December). Available at: https://www.vice.com/en/article/the-freedom-and-beauty-i-found-cruising-for-sex/. (Last accessed: 11 March 2025).

32. Thomas, D. (2024). *Deep Psychology of Kink*, Routledge, pp. 5-6.
33. Stein, S.K. (2021). *Sadomasochism and the BDSM community in the United States kinky people unite.* Routledge, p. 23.
34. Ibid., p. 41.
35. Rubin, G. S. (2011). 'The Catacombs: A Temple of the Butthole', in Rubin, G. S. *Deviations: A Gayle Rubin Reader*. North Carolina, United States: Duke University Press.
36. Sprott, R. and Hadcock, B. B. (2017). 'Bisexuality, pansexuality, queer identity, and kink identity', *Sexual and Relationship Therapy*, 33(2), pp. 1-19. doi: 10.1080/14681994.2017.1347616.
37. Gregory, S. Y. (2024). 'How Queer, Disabled People Are Finding Pleasure and Community Through Kink', *them*, (July). Available at: https://www.them.us/story/queer-disabled-kink-community-spaces. (Last accessed: 11 March 2025).
38. Sagarin, B. J., Cutler, B., Cutler, N., Lawler-Sagarin, K. A., & Matuszewich, L. (2009). Hormonal changes and couple bonding in consensual sadomasochistic activity. *Archives of sexual behavior*, 38(2), pp. 186–200. doi: 10.1007/s10508-008-9374-5.
39. Ambler, J. K., Lee, E. M., Klement, K. R., Loewald, T., Comber, E. M., Hanson, S. A., Cutler, B., Cutler, N., & Sagarin, B. J. (2017). Consensual BDSM facilitates role-specific altered states of consciousness: A preliminary study. *Psychology of Consciousness: Theory, Research, and Practice*, 4(1), pp. 75–91. https://doi.org/10.1037/cns0000097
40. Thomas, D. (2024). *Deep Psychology of Kink*, Routledge, p. 16.
41. Butler, J. (1988). 'Performative Acts and Gender Constitution: An Essay in Phenomenology and Feminist Theory', *Theatre Journal*, 40(4), pp. 519-531.
42. Speciale, M. and Khambatta, D. (2020). 'Kinky & Queer: Exploring the Experiences of LGBTQ + Individuals who Practice BDSM', *Journal of LGBT Issues in Counseling*, 14(4), pp. 341–361. doi: 10.1080/15538605.2020.1827476.
43. Thomas, D. (2024). *Deep Psychology of Kink*, Routledge, p. 9.

44 Cameron, D. (2002). 'History of Our Leather Women's Group in San Francisco', *The Exiles San Francisco*, (December). Available at: https://theexiles.org/history-new/. (Last accessed: 11 March 2025).
45 Atherton Lin, J. (2021). *Gay Bar: Why We Went Out*. UK: Granta Publications, p. 38.
46 As told to me by Pawan Dhall, founder of Kolkata-based Counsel Club, one of India's earliest-known queer support groups.
47 Jyoti, D. (2023). 'How the LGBTQ+ movement grew over the years', *Hindustan Times*, (October). Available at: https://www.hindustantimes.com/india-news/how-the-lgbtq-movement-grew-over-the-years-101697569262901.html. (Last accessed: 11 March 2025).
48 Patel, S. (2018). 'A New Era of the Rise of 'the Other'', *Liberal Studies*, 3(2), p. 173-185.
49 Aronson P. (2008). 'The Markers and Meanings of Growing Up: Contemporary Young Women's Transition from Adolescence to Adulthood', *Gender & society: the official publication of Sociologists for Women in Society*, 22, pp. 56–82. https://doi.org/10.1177/0891243207311420.
50 Atherton Lin, J. (2021). *Gay Bar: Why We Went Out*. UK: Granta Publications, p. 65.
51 Wark, M. (2023). *Raving*. NC: Duke University Press.
52 Baer, H. (2019). *Trans Girl Suicide Museum*. LA: Hesse Press, p. 28.
53 Connolly, D. J., Davies, E., Lynskey, M., Maier, L. J., Ferris, J. A., Barratt, M. J., Winstock, A. R. and Gilchrist G. (2022). 'Differences in Alcohol and Other Drug Use and Dependence Between Transgender and Cisgender Participants from the 2018 Global Drug Survey', *LGBT Health*, 9(8), pp. 534-542. https://doi.org/10.1089/lgbt.2021.0242.
54 Wark, M. (2023). *Raving*. NC: Duke University Press.
55 Locke, K. and Koen, B. D. (2012). 'The Lakota Hoop Dance as Medicine for Social Healing', in Benjamin D. Koen (ed.). *The Oxford Handbook of Medical Ethnomusicology*. UK: Oxford University Press. https://doi.org/10.1093/oxfordhb/9780199756261.001.0001.

56 Ghaziani, A. (2024). *Long Live Queer Nightlife*. NJ: Princeton University Press, p. 4.
57 Tarr, B., Launay J., Cohen E., and Dunbar R. (2015). 'Synchrony and exertion during dance independently raise pain threshold and encourage social bonding', *Biology Letters*, 11: 20150767. doi.org/10.1098/rsbl.2015.0767.
58 Deiana, M. A. (2022). Dance as a register of war: following unruly bodies, affects, and sounds in conflict. *Critical Military Studies*, 9(3), pp. 462–484. https://doi.org/10.1080/23337486.2022.2134139.
59 Muñoz, J. E. (2009). *Cruising Utopia*. NY: NYU Press, p. 1.
60 Ibid., p. 185.
61 Florêncio, J. (2023). 'Chemsex cultures: Subcultural reproduction and queer survival', *Sexualities*, 26(5-6), pp. 556–573.
62 Weinstein, S. (2015). 'Why Clubbing Was Crucial for Gay Men During the AIDS Crisis', *VICE*, (December). Available at: https://www.vice.com/en/article/why-clubbing-was-crucial-for-gay-men-during-the-aids-crisis/. (Last accessed: 11 March 2025).
63 B. M. (2019). 'At the Height of AIDS, San Francisco's Queer Nightlife Became a Refuge', *Them*, (February). Available at: https://www.them.us/story/san-francisco-queer-nightlife-80s-90s. (Last accessed: 11 March 2025).
64 Atherton Lin, J. (2021). *Gay Bar: Why We Went Out*. UK: Granta Publications, p. 66.
65 One Archives at the USC Libraries. *Studio One*. Available at: https://one.usc.edu/archive-location/studio-one-1. (Last accessed: 11 March 2025).
66 Maxwell, K. (2016). 'Racism is rife in the LGBT community. Gay people cannot call for equality while discriminating against others', *The Independent*, (December). Available at: https://www.independent.co.uk/voices/racism-lgbt-gay-rights-equality-discrimination-gay-nightclub-jeremy-joseph-facebook-post-soho-london-shootings-a7501911.html. (Last accessed: 11 March 2025).
67 Glatsky, G. (2021). 'One of the World's Biggest Gay Clubs Has Been Accused of Transphobia', *VICE*, (June). Available

at: https://www.vice.com/en/article/one-of-the-worlds-biggest-gay-clubs-has-been-accused-of-transphobia/. (Last accessed: 11 March 2025).

68   Tapper, J. and Rodney, I. (2024). 'DJs join Ravers for Palestine boycott of top Berlin techno club Berghain', *The Guardian*. Available at: https://www.theguardian.com/world/article/2024/aug/10/djs-join-ravers-for-palestine-boycott-of-top-berlin-techno-club-berghain. (Last accessed: 11 March 2025).

69   Ramsawakh, D. (2018). 'Why accessibility in the queer community is still a problem', *Xtra*, (June). Available at: https://xtramagazine.com/power/why-accessibility-in-the-queer-community-is-still-a-problem-87764. (Last accessed: 11 March 2025).

70   Ghaziani, A. (2014). *There Goes the Gayborhood*. NJ: Princeton University Press.

71   Ghaziani, A. (2024). *Long Live Queer Nightlife*. NJ: Princeton University Press, p. 19-20.

72   Bussy Temple (Howrøng, Minsoo and Zenon) (2024). 'On queer futurity through rave collectives in Southeast Asia', *Mixmag*, (June). Available at: https://mixmag.asia/feature/bussy-temple-queer-futurity-rave-collectives-southeast-asia. (Last accessed: 11 March 2025).

73   Newson, M., Khurana, R., Cazorla, F., and van Mulukom, V. (2021). "I Get High With a Little Help From My Friends' – How Raves Can Invoke Identity Fusion and Lasting Co-operation via Transformative Experiences', *Frontiers in Psychology*, 12(719596). https://doi.org/10.3389/fpsyg.2021.719596.

74   Wilkes, T. (2022). 'In Pictures: The Radical Activism of the UK Gay Liberation Front', *AnOther*, (June). Available at: https://www.anothermag.com/art-photography/14152/queens-jubilee-exhibition-uk-gay-liberation-front-queer-circle-gallery. (Last accessed: 12 March 2025).

75   Green, J. (1988). *Days in the life: voices from the English underground, 1961-1971*. London: Heinemann. Excerpt available at: https://libcom.org/article/origins-gay-liberation-front-and-disrupting-festival-light-uk-1960s. (Last accessed: 12 March 2025).

76. Donohue, C. (2019). 'When Queer Nation 'Bashed Back' Against Homophobia with Street Patrols and Glitter', *KQED*, (June). Available at: https://www.kqed.org/arts/13858167/queer-nation-lgbtq-activism-90s. (Last accessed: 12 March 2025).

77. Lee (2024). 'Infected Faggot Perspectives & dark AIDS humour', *Queer Zine Archive Project*, (July). Available at: https://gittings.qzap.org/tag/act-up/. (Last accessed: 12 March 2025).

78. *Pride*. (2014). Directed by Matthew Warchus. UK: Proud Films, Pathé, BBC Films, British Film Institute, Ingenious Media.

79. Goldhill, S. (2017). 'Play in Ancient Greece'. Interviewed by *American Journal of Play*. *American Journal of Play*, 9(3), pp. 287-298. Available at: https://www.museumofplay.org/app/uploads/2022/01/9-3-interview-1-goldhill.pdf. (Last accessed: 12 March 2025).

80. Noel, A.-S. (2020). 'Play and aesthetics in ancient Greece'. Review of *Play and aesthetics in ancient Greece*, by Stephen E. Kidd. *Bryn Mawr Classical Review*. Available at: https://bmcr.brynmawr.edu/2020/2020.08.11/. (Last accessed: 12 March 2025).

81. Black, H. (2022). 'What Happens when Drag Queens and Beauty Queens Collide?', *Elephant*, (August). Available at: https://elephant.art/what-happens-when-drag-queens-and-beauty-queens-collide-16082022/. (Last accessed: 12 March 2025).

82. Lake, B. and Orloff, A. (1996). *The Unsinkable Bambi Lake*. SF: Manic D Press.

83. Ghaziani, A. (2024). *Long Live Queer Nightlife*. NJ: Princeton University Press, p. 19.

84. Kinywa, B. (2024). 'The Joy and Resilience of Kenya's First Kiki Ball', *i-D*, (September). Available at: https://i-d.co/article/nairobi-ballroom-report-voguing-haus-of-andeti/. (Last accessed: 12 March 2025).

85. Sontag, S. (1966). 'Notes on 'Camp'', in Sontag, S. *Against Interpretation: And Other Essays*. NY: Dell Pub.

86. Medhurst, E. (2021). 'Lesbian Feminist Dress Codes', *Dressing Dykes*, 30 July. Available at: https://dressingdykes.

com/2021/07/30/lesbian-feminist-dress-codes/. (Last accessed: 12 March 2025).

87 Halberstam, J. (1999). 'Oh Bondage, Up Yours! Female Masculinity and the Tomboy', in Rottnek, M. (ed.) *Sissies and Tomboys: Gender Nonconformity and Homosexual Childhood*. NY: NYU Press, pp. 153-179.

88 *Queendom*. (2023). Directed by Agniia Galdanova. France-US: Inmaat Productions, Doc Society, Sundance Institute, Vancouver Film School.

89 Castle, T. in *The Female Closet*. (1998). Directed by Barbara Hammer. US: Barbara Hammer.

90 Muchado, C. M. (2020). *In the Dream House*. UK: Serpent's Tail.

91 Caswell, M., Cifor, M., Ramirez, M. H. (2016). '"To Suddenly Discover Yourself Existing": Uncovering the Impact of Community Archives', *The American Archivist*, 79(1), pp. 56–81. https://doi.org/10.17723/0360-9081.79.1.56.

92 Malik, N. (2023). 'What does it mean to erase a people – a nation, culture, identity? In Gaza, we are beginning to find out', *The Guardian*, (December). Available at: https://www.theguardian.com/commentisfree/2023/dec/18/gaza-israel-destroying-culture-and-identity. (Last accessed: 12 March 2025).

93 Schillace, B. (2021). 'The Forgotten History of the World's First Trans Clinic', *Scientific American*, (May). Available at: https://www.scientificamerican.com/article/the-forgotten-history-of-the-worlds-first-trans-clinic/. (Last accessed: 12 March 2025).

94 National Galleries of Scotland (2022). *The Queer Code: Secret Languages of LGBTQ+ Art*. [Online video]. Available at: https://www.youtube.com/watch?v=w447WOQZNNQ. (Last accessed: 12 March 2025).

95 Dyke Action Machine (2008). *About DAM*. Available at: https://www.dykeactionmachine.com/about/page7.html. (Last accessed: 12 March 2025).

96 Ibid.

97 Barua, M. (2020). 'The Past and Present of Queer Art in India through Bhupen Khakhar's Paintings', *Mezosfera*, (August). Available at: http://mezosfera.org/the-past-and-

present-of-queer-art-in-india-through-bhupen-khakhars-paintings/. (Last accessed: 12 March 2025).

98 Maholi, Z. (2023). 'Zanele Muholi: Unflinching images that confront injustice', Interviewed by Precious Adesina. *BBC Culture*. 9th February. Available at: https://www.bbc.com/culture/article/20230208-zanele-muholi-unflinching-images-that-confront-injustice. (Last accessed: 12 March 2025).

99 Vickhoff, B., Malmgren H., Åström R., *et al.* (2013). 'Music structure determines heart rate variability of singers', *Frontiers in Psychology*, 4(334). doi:10.3389/fpsyg.2013.00334.

100 Lindenberger, U., Li, S. C., Gruber, W. *et al.* (2009). 'Brains swinging in concert: cortical phase synchronization while playing guitar', *BMC Neurosci*, 10(22). https://doi.org/10.1186/1471-2202-10-22.

101 Sontag, S. (1966). 'Our Culture and the New Sensibility', in Sontag, S. *Against Interpretation: And Other Essays*. NY: Dell Pub.

102 *Rebel Dykes*. (2021). Directed by Harri Shanahan and Siân A. Williams. UK: Siobhan Fahey.

103 Feather, S. (2015). *Blowing the Lid: Gay Liberation, Sexual Revolution and Radical Queens*, UK: Zero Books, p. 458.

104 Bishopsgate Institute (1971). *Gay Liberation Front manifesto, London, 1971*. London. Available at: https://s3.eu-west-1.amazonaws.com/bishopsgate/GLF-Manifesto-1971.pdf?mtime=20220707134248. (Last accessed: 12 March 2025).

105 hooks, b. (1999). *All About Love*. NY: HarperCollins.

106 Levin, N. J., Kattari, S. K., Piellusch, E. K., Wats, E. (2020). '"We Just Take Care of Each Other": Navigating 'Chosen Family' in the Context of Health, Illness, and the Mutual Provision of Care amongst Queer and Transgender Young Adults', *International Journal of Environmental Research and Public Health*, 17(19). doi:10.3390/ijerph17197346.

107 Halberstam, J. (2005). *In a Queer Time and Place: Transgender Bodies, Subcultural Lives*. NY and London: NYU Press.

108 Weston, K. (1997). *Families We Choose: Lesbians, Gays, Kinship*. Revised edition. NY: Columbia University Press.

109 Levin, N. J., Kattari, S. K., Piellusch, E. K., Wats, E. (2020). '"We Just Take Care of Each Other": Navigating 'Chosen Family' in the Context of Health, Illness, and the Mutual

Provision of Care amongst Queer and Transgender Young Adults', *International Journal of Environmental Research and Public Health*, 17(19). doi:10.3390/ijerph17197346.
110 Mejía, C.E. (2015). 'Mixed-Status Latinx Families: Love and Chosen Family as a Means of Resistance to the American Dream', *Tapestries: Interwoven voices of local and global identities*, 4(1:16).
111 Stack, C. (1974). *All our kin: Strategies for survival in a black community*. NY: Harper and Row.
112 Women's Museum of California (2019). *The Blood Sisters of San Diego*. Available at: https://womensmuseum.wordpress.com/2019/04/10/the-blood-sisters-of-san-diego/. (Last accessed: 12 March 2025).
113 Arnold, E. A., & Bailey, M. M. (2009). Constructing Home and Family: How the Ballroom Community Supports African American GLBTQ Youth in the Face of HIV/AIDS, *Journal of gay & lesbian social services*, 21(2-3), pp. 171–188. https://doi.org/10.1080/10538720902772006.
114 Gonsalves, G. S., Mayer, K. and Beyrer, C. (2022). 'Déjà vu All Over Again? Emergent Monkeypox, Delayed Responses, and Stigmatized Populations', *J Urban Health*, 99, pp. 603–606. https://doi.org/10.1007/s11524-022-00671-.
115 Arefin, M. N. (2021). *Mapping Alternative Futures through Fungi: The Usefulness of Mycorrhizal Networks as a Metaphor for Mutual Aid*. Science, Technology and Society MSc. University College London. Available at: https://www.researchgate.net/publication/359294856_Mapping_Alternative_Futures_through_Fungi_The_Usefulness_of_Mycorrhizal_Networks_as_a_Metaphor_for_Mutual_Aid. (Last accessed: 12 March 2025).
116 Fan, A. (2024). 'More Than a Techno Club: Bassiani as a Political Frontier of Georgia', *Berkeley Political Review*, (February). Available at: https://bpr.studentorg.berkeley.edu/2024/02/14/more-than-a-techno-club-bassiani-as-a-political-frontier-of-georgia/. (Last accessed: 12 March 2025).
117 Horoom Nights (2023). 5 April. Available at: https://www.instagram.com/p/CqqEfzkM6hI/?hl=en (Last accessed: 12 March 2025).

118 Stroude, W. (2021). 'Inside Tbilisi's politically-charged underground queer scene', *Attitude*, (July). Available at: https://www.attitude.co.uk/life/travel/inside-tbilisis-politically-charged-underground-queer-scene-303263/. (Last accessed: 12 March 2025).

119 Simard, S., Perry, D., Jones, M., *et al.* (1997). 'Net transfer of carbon between tree species with shared ectomycorrhizal fungi', *Nature*, 388, pp. 579-582.

120 Camp Trans (2025). *About*. Available at: https://www.camptrans.uk/about (Last accessed: 12 March 2025).

121 AHUS (2024). 30 April. Available at https://www.instagram.com/americahatesus/p/C6XS0lcS7oF/?img_index=1 (Last accessed: 12 March 2025)

122 Hagstrom, A., Betz, B. and Mion, L. (2024). 'Antisemitic agitators rage on at campuses across the country', *Fox News*, (April). Available at: https://www.foxnews.com/live-news/april-28-campus-antisemitic-israel-agitators-protest-columbia. (Last accessed: 12 March 2025)

123 Gattuso, R. (2019). 'How Lesbian Potlucks Nourished the LGBTQ Movement', *Gastro Obscura*, (May). Available at: https://www.atlasobscura.com/articles/why-do-lesbians-have-potlucks-on-pride. (Last accessed: 12 March 2025).

124 Lorde, A. (1983). Interviewed by Claudia Tate. *Black Women Writers at Work*. NY: Continuum.

125 Gattuso, R. (2019). 'How Lesbian Potlucks Nourished the LGBTQ Movement', *Gastro Obscura*, (May). Available at: https://www.atlasobscura.com/articles/why-do-lesbians-have-potlucks-on-pride. (Last accessed: 12 March 2025).

126 Smith, B. (1989). 'A Press of Our Own Kitchen Table: Women of Color Press', *Frontiers: A Journal of Women Studies*, 10(3), pp. 11-13.

127 Beauvoir, S. de. (2009). *The Second Sex*. UK: Jonathan Cape.

128 Lorde, A. (1979). 'The Master's Tools Will Never Dismantle the Master's House', in *Sister Outsider: Essays and Speeches*. CA: Crossing Press, pp. 110-114.

129 Wu, T. (2018). 'The Tyranny of Convenience', *The New York Times*, (February). Available at: https://www.nytimes.com/2018/02/16/opinion/sunday/tyranny-convenience.html. (Last accessed: 13 March 2025).

130 Atshan, S. (2020). *Queer Palestine and the Empire of Critique*. CA: Stanford University Press.
131 Yurcaba, J. (2025). 'Government agencies scrub LGBTQ web pages and remove info about trans and intersex people', *NBC News*, (February). Available at: https://www.nbcnews.com/nbc-out/out-politics-and-policy/government-agencies-scrub-lgbtq-web-pages-remove-info-trans-intersex-p-rcna190519. (Last accessed: 13 March 2025).
132 Archie, A. and Diaz, J. (2025). 'Trump signs an order restricting gender-affirming care for people under 19', *NPR*, (January). Available at: https://www.npr.org/2025/01/29/nx-s1-5279092/trump-executive-order-gender-affirming-care. (Last accessed: 13 March 2025).
133 Hunter Schafer (2025) 21 February. Available at: https://www.tiktok.com/@csbvkjbvjkbkjjvkfsjk/video/7473999740842151214?lang=en. (Last accessed: 13 March 2025).
134 McKetta, S., Hoatson, T., Hughes, L. D. *et al.* (2024). 'Disparities in Mortality by Sexual Orientation in a Large, Prospective Cohort of Female Nurses', *JAMA*, 331(19), pp. 1638-1645. doi: 10.1001/jama.2024.4459.
135 The Trevor Project (2024). 'Perceived Life Expectancy and Life Purpose in LGBTQ+ Young People'. Available at: https://www.thetrevorproject.org/research-briefs/perceived-life-expectancy-and-life-purpose-in-lgbtq-young-people/. (Last accessed: 13 March 2025).
136 Kohrt, B. A., Ottman, K., Panter-Brick, C. *et al.* (2020). 'Why we heal: The evolution of psychological healing and implications for global mental health', *Clinical Psychology Review*, 82. https://doi.org/10.1016/j.cpr.2020.101921.
137 Darley, J. M. and Latane, B. (1968). 'Bystander intervention in emergencies: Diffusion of responsibility', *Journal of Personality and Social Psychology*, 8(4, Pt. 1), pp. 377-383. https://doi.org.10.1037/h0025589.
138 Wark, M. (2023). 'Critical (Autho) Theory', *e-flux Journal*, 140. Available at: https://www.e-flux.com/jhttps://www.sciencedirect.com/science/article/pii/S0272735820301082ournal/140/572300/critical-auto-theory/. (Last accessed: 13 March 2025).

Acknowledgements

Thank you to the incredible Heather McDaid and Laura Jones-Rivera at 404 Ink for believing in this book, and for their patience and incisive editorial guidance. And thank you to Luke Bird for manifesting the hottest book cover, a deliciously aesthetic delight.

My chosen family. Without the [redacted] Commune holding me close these past four years, I would never have been able to birth this baby into the big wide world. To have grown through my mid-'20s with you is a privilege I don't take lightly.

Thank you, my darling Gus, it's been so FUN. Thank you for seeing me deeply – for supporting me in healing, growth and insecurity – and for helping me learn more about love every day.

And to my mum and Paul for literally everything (but specifically for teaching me how to research!).

This is an ode to all the queer artists, ravers, fighters who have sunlit my days, curated my nights and soundtracked my life. This is in memory of every trans kid who never got to grow up. And of Sophie Williams, taken too soon, whose care for the community changed my life.

Finally, thank you to the lovers with whom I play, and to James for the hedono-futurism. Mwah! xo

About the Author

Photo credit: Eivind Hansen

Prishita (they/them) is interested in the historical, personal, and political stories of the queer community, and has written extensively on these matters while drawing on their experiences as an LGBTQ+ rights campaigner and community organiser. Previously Politics Editor at BRICKS Magazine, they have by-lines in *Gay Times*, *gal-dem*, *Dazed*, *Metal*, and *Cosmopolitan*, among others. Prishita has also written for a range of scientific publications, including *Triple Helix Cambridge*, and is a co-author on a paper on the second plague pandemic published in Nature Communications.

About the Inklings series

This book is part of 404 Ink's Inkling series which presents big ideas in pocket-sized books.

They are all available at 404ink.com/shop.

If you enjoyed this book, you may also enjoy these titles in the series:

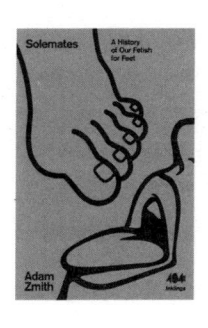

Solemates – Adam Zmith
Solemates brings to light the history of this peculiarly popular kink. From Tarantino films to Bible stories, from Renaissance paintings to OnlyFans, Solemates is the rich and messy tale of our obsession with everything below the ankle, and what it reveals about how we view our bodies and our sex lives.

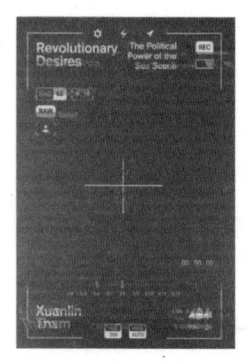

Revolutionary Desires – Xuanlin Tham

Cinema is becoming less and less sexy; yet more and more people are rallying against sex on screen. Why is the sex scene, demonised as it is, therefore more politically important and subversive than ever? *Revolutionary Desires* seeks to answer that question.

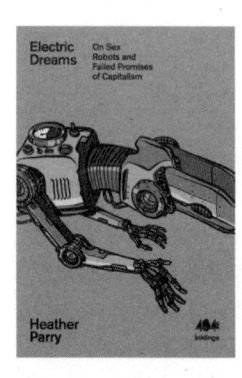

Electric Dreams – Heather Parry

Why are sex robots such a hot topic? *Electric Dreams* picks apart the forces that posit sex robots as either the solution to our problems or a real threat to human safety, and looks at what's being pushed aside for us to obsess about something that will never happen.